William G. Don

Reminiscences of the Baltic Fleet of 1855

William G. Don

Reminiscences of the Baltic Fleet of 1855

ISBN/EAN: 9783337296339

Printed in Europe, USA, Canada, Australia, Japan

Cover: Foto ©ninafisch / pixelio.de

More available books at **www.hansebooks.com**

REMINISCENCES

OF THE

BALTIC FLEET

OF 1855.

BY

WILLIAM GERARD DON, M.D.,

DEPUTY SURGEON - GENERAL.

PRINTED, NOT PUBLISHED.

D. H. EDWARDS, ADVERTISER OFFICE, BRECHIN.

1894.

Dedicated

TO THOSE OF MY FRIENDS WHO,
JUDICIOUSLY OR OTHERWISE,
INDUCED ME TO PRINT THESE
REMINISCENCES.

W. G. Don.

PREFACE.

THE following reminiscences have been compiled from a Journal kept by me while serving in the Baltic Fleet, supplemented by recollections which had not, and never can fade from my memory.

While mixing in other scenes, during thirty years of military service in various parts of the world, the very existence of the Journal (which was carefully preserved by my dear mother) had almost passed from my mind.

Yet, in perusing it, to recast the following summary, most of the events recorded came back with surprising clearness, not merely in the main, but even in detail—proving, indeed, that youthful impressions are stamped on the memory with a permanence withheld from those of riper years.

The personal incidents here given are faithfully recorded; while those more hearsay are of a most trustworthy kind. For, being in the Flagship, I always had information at first hand, through my good friend Paymaster Munday, Secretary to the Admiral; as well as access to official charts, plans, and lists, and so had the best knowledge alike of our own and the French Squadron, as of Russian ships, forts, and fortresses.

After the lapse of forty years I am able to write of these matters, as well as to mention shipmates by name, in a way impossible for the first decade or two following the events described. The events have long since been public property, and the actors therein, alas! nearly all beyond either praise or censure. Of the latter there is none, because there was none to give.

This book is only for my family and friends, to whom I feel it will be acceptable.

For imperfections in method and manner, I crave indulgence; for the matter itself I need offer no apology.

W. G. DON.

52 CANFIELD GARDENS,
    WEST HAMPSTEAD,
        LONDON, N.W.

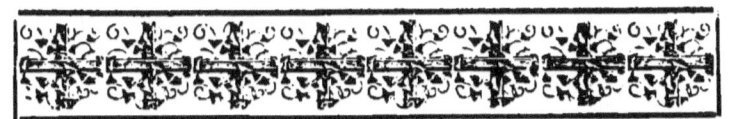

CONTENTS.

	PAGE
CHAPTER I.	
Volunteering,	9-15
CHAPTER II.	
Portsmouth,	16-21
CHAPTER III.	
Join the Fleet,	22-30
CHAPTER IV.	
Life on the "Duke,"	31-36
CHAPTER V.	
Routine of a War Ship,	37-41
CHAPTER VI.	
Shipmates,	42-49
CHAPTER VII.	
Rendezvous at Kiel,	50-56
CHAPTER VIII.	
Revel and Nargen,	57-64
CHAPTER IX.	
Cronstadt,	65-72
CHAPTER X.	
Infernal Machines,	73-81
CHAPTER XI.	
Preparations against Sweaborg,	82-94

CHAPTER XII.
Bombardment of Sweaborg, - - - - 95-105
CHAPTER XIII.
Post Bombardment, - - - - -106-114
CHAPTER XIV.
Homeward Bound, - - - - - -115-121
APPENDIX.
Some of our Baltic Gun Room Songs, - -123-129
Index, - - - - - - - -131-138

Reminiscences of the Baltic Fleet of 1855.

CHAPTER I.

VOLUNTEERING.

THE Baltic Fleet, which, under Admiral Sir Richard Dundas, assembled at Spithead in March 1855, was, in many respects, much stronger, better manned, and more thoroughly equipped than that of 1854, under Sir Charles Napier. It had, especially, many more small craft —particularly gun and mortar boats—requiring a relatively larger complement of officers and men ; notably of medical officers. But of the latter, as in wars before and since, afloat and ashore there was a serious deficiency.

It was at the time simply impossible to get a sufficient number of fully qualified young medical men for the navy ; for Turkey and the Crimea had already absorbed all those available. The Government, therefore, in order to provide medical aid for the numerous vessels of the Baltic Fleet, had

B

resort, as in the wars with France during the early part of the century, to the temporary employment of medical students of a certain standing and qualification, under letters of service as " Hospital Dressers ;" or, as the sailors themselves, in traditional and far happier nautical language called them, " Doctor's Mates."

The writer was one of them.

One fine day towards the end of March, 1855, when upwards of a hundred and fifty third year students were assembled in the Surgical Theatre of the Edinburgh Infirmary, in the Clinical Class of the celebrated Professor James Syme, that most practical of men, of few words but great works, startled us by the unusual announcement that he had something very important to say at the end of the lecture. When that was finished, he quietly drew from his pocket a big official letter, in which he read that the Admiralty were prepared to employ, temporarily, in the Baltic Fleet, forty third year students of Edinburgh, whom he—Syme —could recommend. The terms were: the then ordinary pay (7s 6d per diem) of an Assistant Surgeon; to wear undress with sword; to mess in the gunroom ; to be discharged and sent home in time to resume studies next winter. Syme simply said:—" This, gentlemen, may prove no holiday service; those wishing to volunteer must hand in their names now to me, and they will be told to-morrow whether they are accepted. All I can say is, I wish I was young enough to go myself.'

Such a laconic appeal from the plucky old professor proved irresistible: it was followed by a short buzz of conversation, then a shout, and a simultaneous leap over seats into the amphitheatre of about eighty students to give in their names;

it was pure impulse without hesitation or reflection.

Needless to say, none of the volunteers did any more work that day; we felt as if already actually and irretrievably enlisted; and could only think of the morrow with excited impatience. At noon next day the names of the forty chosen were posted up, amid the wild excitement of those accepted, and the chill disappointment of the rejected.

But our enthusiasm was somewhat checked and sobered when we were told we must start for London in a few days, to which railway passes would be provided; for it meant to the majority of the volunteers only bare time to communicate by letter with those near and dear, and none to go home any distance and say good-bye! We now began to realise we were actually going on service of certain risk, and perhaps great danger, without having sought or obtained the consent of parents or gaurdians, or even bidding them a personal farewell! At the time, I felt my behaviour towards my old mother was most undutiful, and have often since looked back doubtfully on the essentially madcap and reckless character of our proceedings during those few days. But the buoyancy of youth and inexperience kept us up; and we were by no means unaware that, as the war fever then ran high in the country, we would be supported by general and popular approval.

So, with light hearts, merely touched by passing sadness, or misgiving, all we had time for was to write a few hurried family letters; pack up what we did not seem to want; and prepare to start, with an attenuated kit, like newly enlisted runaways, off and away on an enterprise of which none of us had the smallest knowledge or experience whatever.

When the evening for departure arrived, there was a large muster of friends at the Waverley Station to see us off by the ordinary night train to London. We were a noisy lot, and the usual passengers gave us a wide berth; so that whole compartments were rapidly filled by college chums. In the one I was in, however, there was a stray middle-aged Scotsman returning to his English home; and being a jolly and tolerant fellow, evidently prepared to be one of us.

Away we started amid great cheering, and at once began to kill the journey in our own hilarious fashion; our outsider presently gave us "The Englishman," with so much acceptance that he had to sing it several times; and thus was heard, all the way to York, even above the roar of the train, songs and choruses, given as only wild and excited students can. During a halt at York we invaded the refreshment rooms like a pack of hungry wolves; but I slipped from the eating and drinking hubbub, and peered out of the station into the darkness, to try and catch even the outline of the grand old Minster, in which I was happily successful.

The singing was resumed, even with increased vigour, when we started again: but gradually subsided as we dropped off to sleep, one by one, exhausted; it was recommenced, however, when the cold grey dawn aroused us, and kept up in tolerable blast until we reached King's Cross.

London, in its vastness, was entirely new to all my immediate party, except Coghill, who, having betimes lived in it, said, or pretended, he could pilot us about everywhere. Under his guidance eight of us found ourselves presently at "Sam's Coffee House" in the Strand.

That old hostel—long since swept out of existence—was small and stuffy; and everything, from furniture to waiters, ancient and seedy. Its culinary resources did not go beyond plain joints, chops, steaks, fish, ham and eggs; but what it supplied was good. It was good enough for us; for at that time there was little better outside the big hotels; and, excepting "Simpson's," not a single restaurant or buffet of the modern type in all London.

Our orders were to present ourselves before the Naval Medical Director General at Somerset House, with certificates as vouchers of identity in our hands, to tally with those already forwarded by Syme through the post.

After a wash up, and breakfast of ham and eggs, we crossed the street to Somerset House at twelve o'clock, and found our fellow-volunteers from Edinburgh, as well as about thirty from London, mustered in the waiting room. Presently we were individually interviewed by a very sharp, dark, dapper little man, Dr Bryson, Medical Naval Director General, who directed our return at the same hour next day, when we would learn our fate. On re-assembling, my own name was the very first called by the usher, and on confronting the Director General, he abruptly asked what ship I would like to be appointed to? Ship? I had never seen a man-of-war, except the guardship at Queensferry; but a happy inspiration made me say "the Flagship." And so, by a kind of accident, fruitful of pleasant results to myself, I received a letter of appointment to the magnificent "Duke of Wellington, 131 guns," the largest wooden three-decker afloat, before or since. My satisfaction was much increased on learning that my friend and fellow Edinburgh volunteer, James More, had also been appointed to the "Duke."

In a similar manner a certain number of volunteers were given choice of ships; but the majority were posted without being consulted, and some of the London men altogether rejected, even at the eleventh hour.

We were then informed by an official that each would receive an advance of £25, to provide uniform and a sea kit; that the former could be best got in London, and the latter in Portsmouth. In discussing where best to get uniform, the indefatigable Coghill again came to the rescue, and promptly introduced our party to his relative, Mr Mackay, of Mackay, Burke & Wheeler, tailors, New Bond Street. By that enterprising firm we had a satisfactory rig out in a few days. Mr Mackay was a somewhat battered Scotsman of middle life, and festively inclined; and so, to show his appreciation of our custom, invited us to supper in the new, and then wonderful Canterbury Hall. We were much struck with the novelty of having supper in the body of the hall while the entertainment was going on; and I remember, while the devilled kidneys and baked potatoes were before us, the favourite and famous Sam Cowell, whom we had before known in Edinburgh, came forward and sang "Billy Barlow"—the last time I was destined to hear him.

Having got uniform, and received official letters of appointment to our respective ships, we were furnished with railway passes to Portsmouth, and directed to join at once.

Accordingly, on the 26th of March, we left

Waterloo Station in select parties; mine consisted of Lees, Scott, Wallace, and myself. We were no longer the roystering and boisterous students of the journey to London; but in our own estimation young gentlemen of considerably enhanced importance and dignity, actually proceeding to join as officers in Her Majesty's Navy!

As we passed Farnborough, we noticed Aldershot Camp, then in process of formation on the barren heath. It looked a wretched spot, and little did I think that in after life I should spend some of my best years in that apparently uninviting locality.

CHAPTER II.

PORTSMOUTH.

ON arrival at Portsmouth we put up at the Pier Hotel, on the well-known Common Hard.

I had resolved to keep a Journal or Diary, —or in more appropriate nautical language, a Log ; and the first thing done in Portsmouth was the purchase of a book suitable for the purpose. I selected a thick foolscap volume, bound in white sheep's skin, which is now before me in excellent preservation. Although the front binding is somewhat abraded, it is still visibly adorned with finely executed pen and ink naval emblems by Lees, himself a born artist, as well as the son of an artist— his father being Mr Lees, historical painter and whilom Secretary of the Royal Scottish Academy. In the centre is an anchor; on the right a stalwart British tar of the period, waving a union jack; at his feet, a pile of cannon shot with a rifle and cutlass : overhead a rammer and sponge crossed ; a sailor's hat in one corner, and a marine's shako in the other. It bears the legend " Duke of Wellington 131 guns, Baltic 1855." On the back binding is inscribed, " Baltic Expedition. The Log—1855."

As the number of guns carried by the Duke was prominently, and even proudly, often stated in my Journal, the fact was seized, on my return home, by my waggish brother Henry, as a ready subject for banter; and I often found "131 guns," scribbled on my letters, on the walls, the soles of my morning boots—anywhere, everywhere to catch the eye. The chaff was in no way incongenial to me.

I began my Journal—March 26th—the very night of the purchase of the book ; and continued it daily throughout my naval career with commendable care and precision. It is also illustrated with a few rude sketches of Russian ships, forts and towns, as well as tracings of maps and plans of Cronstadt and Sweaborg. Lastly, I jotted down the words of some popular songs, which we sang nightly in the Gunroom.

We had supper, retired early, and were aroused at 5 a.m. by the morning gun from the " Victory," which somewhat rude awakening we considered our first introduction to naval life. As daylight came in, we caught eagerly from the hotel windows the hazy outline of the mighty Fleet at Spithead, which was the goal of our hopes. After breakfast, we watched the novel and extraordinary amenities of a great naval port, such as then witnessed on the historic " Hard." We proceeded to don our uniforms, for the first time officially, and it was a proud sensation to buckle on a sword which one was now actually entitled to wear! Duly attired, and with appointment letters in hand, we proceeded to the pier about 11 a.m., hired a boat, and set out to join our respective ships. We rowed round the " Victory " and were speedily out of the inner harbour, when a truly marvellous sight was unfolded ; the water, smooth as glass, was literally covered for miles with all sorts of naval and civil craft passing to and from the mighty ships looming in the distance. Our boatman made direct for the Flagship, and at noon I stepped upon the upper deck of the magnificent "Duke," followed by my comrades. We were much astonished at the swarming multitude of men 'tween decks, then about to sit down to dinner. I inquired for Assistant Surgeon George Duncan, whose name I had got hold of, and that bluff but kindly Aberdonian at once put me up to the ropes. I reported myself to Captain Henry Caldwell, who courteously asked a few questions, and directed the Paymaster to enroll my name in the ship's books. Here was indeed a proud moment for a green and beardless country lad of nineteen, which I thus recorded in my Journal:

"I discovered myself one of the officers of the Duke of Wellington, and no longer a subject merely, but a servant of the Queen as well"!

Having fully ascertained what articles of sea kit were required, I got shore leave for three days to complete outfit. We then left in our boat for Wallace's ship the "Cæsar, 91 guns," a splendid new two decker; then to Lee's ship the "Nile, 91 guns," a two decker of an older type : and, lastly, to Scott's ship the "Cressy, 80 guns," also a two decker of a still earlier build. These gentlemen having reported themselves, and obtained leave the same as myself, we returned ashore together, deeply impressed with our first visit to one of the most powerful fleets which up to that time had ever assembled at Spithead.

The date of our actual joining was Tuesday, March 27th, 1855.

The next three days were spent hunting up sea kit and exploring Portsmouth. None of us had any previous experience of an English provincial town, much less of a naval port, and so everything was absolutely new. Accustomed as we had been to the stately stone streets of Edinburgh, we thought Portsmouth, with its narrow crooked thoroughfares and small dingy brick houses, one of the meanest of places; the absence of landmarks, and the curious ramifications of moats and fortifications, made it also very confusing ; but we fully recognised that, however unprepossessing, it was then probably the liveliest place in the world. The motley crowds that thronged its narrow thoroughfares were a sight to see. In addition to a big normal civil population, and a large military garrison, there was also a heavy contingent of the twenty thousand men of the Fleet always on shore; vast numbers of visitors, too—friends and relatives of the sailors, and shoals of more than doubtful male and female characters were afoot, who had flocked from London and the provinces in the hope of picking up something. Every fifth or sixth person in the street was a soldier or a sailor in uniform. In its time Portsmouth has been the centre of many stirring scenes, but probably never before had such a large and heterogenous collection of humanity been within its area as at that time.

Buying a sea kit was indeed a new experience. Lees and I freely exploited the poky and stuffy shops of the marine dealers, who were mostly Jews, and hard to drive a bargain with. The first requisite was a hold-all "sea chest," and I secured, second hand, an enormously heavy one, built of the stoutest timber, with huge rope handles. It looked, and probably dated from the days of Nelson : for it had been sorely battered, torn, and indented in many a stirring cruise, yet was, nevertheless, still sound and sea worthy. It would be just as impossible for a modern carpenter to construct such a chest as it would be for him to build an old fashioned 74 liner. It measured about four feet long, by half as many broad and deep, and into it all I possessed had to be packed, for it was the only package besides the hammock allowed on board. Our kit included a metal wash basin, metal tumbler, towels, soap, looking glass, and other toilet requisites; blacking and brushes, spare boots, rubber shoes for wet decks, and other small articles. For the hammock, a mattress, pillow, sheets and blankets; and in lieu of a counterpane, I bought a warm woollen horse rug!

Having completed purchases, and stowed them into our capacious chests, we finally doffed our civilian clothes, and I packed mine into a portmanteau, left with my friend, Mr Maclean of the Customs Department, whose acquaintance I had previously made when he was stationed in Aberdeen.

Our last day on shore brought with it much food for reflection; the rumoured speedy sailing of the Fleet had sent crowds of officers and men on shore to complete purchases, have a last fling, and say good-bye to sweethearts and wives. The scenes we then witnessed baffled description: the human medley seemed more heterogeneous than ever; everywhere sounds of music, dancing, drinking, laughing, weeping, swearing, and even praying; the height of mirth and the depth of grief side by side; recklessness blended with prudence; piety mixed with ribaldry, profanity with prayer; thieves, cheap-jacks, mountebanks, and preachers shouted against each other!

The feelings and sentiments of the participators

in the scene were, doubtless, as mixed and varied as the medley itself. The men of the Fleet must all, in greater or less degree, have realised they were proceeding on service of which none could estimate the peril, or foretell who might return. Yet, individually the out look was very different; the gay young sailor kissing his "Polly" was in quite a different position from the sedate married man embracing his weeping wife, and clinging children — perhaps for the last time! Such reflections were readily suggested to the onlooker.

The scene was altogether one only to be paralleled and called forth on the departure of a great Fleet in time of war, none who saw it could forget it!

CHAPTER III.

JOIN THE FLEET.

ON Saturday, March 31st, I embarked for duty; but, at the ship's side, before my chest and bedding could be hoisted on board, I had to go through the formality of obtaining the permission of the First Lieutenant, after which it was swung up, and speedily deposited in the cockpit, under the hooks where my hammock was to swing nightly. The top of the chest and the hammock were to constitute my private residence for the next six months.

I personally reported my arrival on board to the Commander—Preedy—who had the reputation of being a tartar, but was in reality a frank and hearty sailor.

My colleague, More, shortly afterwards turned up, and was located near me.

My introduction to the Gun Room was devoid of the smallest formality, and I had not the least difficulty in making the acquaintance of my messmates, who were all as frank and free with each other as members of a family.

A Marine named Hamblin, a thoroughly knowing old "Joey" of some fifteen years' service, was told off as my servant; whose duty it was to sling and unsling the hammock morning and evening, bring water, brush boots and clothes, and generally act the part of a valet. According to my after experience of soldier servants, he was a very good one.

After tea, and plenty of it, at 6 o'clock, feeling tired, I turned in early; and on going below found Hamblin, with everything in order, waiting for me. He politely asked if there were any more commands, and wished me a good night in my new surroundings.

I had a real, genuine night's rest, and awoke on Sunday, April 1st, feeling anything but a fool: my first thoughts were how very comfortable a hammock is! It is true, one lies somewhat doubled up, and there is less free play for the limbs than in a four poster, but, if the weather be cool, it is distinctly preferable to a hard ship's bunk. I turned out at 7 A.M., the hour at which the officers' hammocks have to be unslung, and carried to the netting on the quarter deck. The faithful Hamblin was here to the minute, and had everything in the programme of my toilet spread out ready on the lid of the chest. Fortunately, my beard then required little shaving; for, in the dim light of the cockpit, that operation was carried on more by touch than sight. My mates all turned out at the same time; but already the whole ship was instinct with life and bustle. Overhead, the decks were being holystoned, scrubbed, slashed, swabbed, with a medley accompaniments of whistling, shouting, singing, and swearing.

Presently, the ship's band tuned up, and played lively airs on the quarter deck. My Scottish notions of the fitness of things were undergoing a rude transformation, and, says I to myself, can this be a Sabbath morning?

By breakfast time the entire ship was as clean

as a new pin, and orderly as sweet. After the usual divisional muster, I was introduced to my far from onerous sick bay duties. The drums then beat to church parade on the middle deck, where forms were placed on the one side for the bluejackets, and the other for the marines ; chairs were placed on the port side for the senior, and starboard for the junior officers, and the pulpit set up between.

Catholics and Dissenters were not bound to attend. The service was read by the Chaplain, Mr Onslow, but he did not preach. Nothing could exceed the decorum of the parade, but with the " Amen" of the blessing disappeared every vestige of what I had been accustomed to associate with a Sunday.

The ship was immediately thrown open, and hundreds of visitors, of both sexes, and of all ages and conditions, swarmed on board from the boats which already thronged around. By the afternoon the decks resembled a country fair. By evening the general liveliness of the crew made it evident that the visitors had not come on board empty handed ! The scene to me all day was of much interest, and altogether I was very favourably impressed with the heartiness, kindness, and good humour to be seen on every side.

Especially was I satisfied with my mess and messmates ; for a Sunday dinner is always an extra good one. I recorded that it included roast veal and mutton, boiled beef, pork chops, plum pudding, apple tart, etc., and the question occurred to me, Can this be a normal feeding ? Where is the traditional salt junk and plum " duff " usually reckoned the staple on board a man o' war ? I learned when it came in afterwards.

When the day ended and our visitors had departed, we still had a huge population left ; for I record that the ship's company sleeping on board that night numbered 1,700 men.

My duties not being very exigent, I obtained leave to visit Portsmouth, chiefly to see my friend, Mr Maclean, through whom I hoped to receive some small articles from home.

When on shore I came across friend Giraud, who had been appointed to the "Malacca," 17 guns, which was being fitted for service in the White Sea, where he hoped to pick up lots of prize money. She had just landed sick and wounded from the Crimea, and, when he took me on board, looked so frightfully dirty and uncomfortable, that I would not have changed places with him for any amount of prospective prize money.

I returned to the "Duke" with a party about eight o'clock, in a dark, dirty night, with a half-drunk boatman, who entertained us with an account of the upsetting of a boat visiting the "Nile" that day, but none were "drownded."

On April 3rd I took stock of the Fleet, then riding in two lines at Spithead, as follows :—

	CAPTAINS.
"Duke of Wellington," screw, the largest three decker in the world, 131 guns. Flagship of Sir Richard S. Dundas, Commodore Pelham, staff, ...	Henry Caldwell.
"Royal George," screw, three decker, 101 guns, ...	Eyres.
"Neptune," sailing, three decker, 120 guns,...	Hutton.
"Exmouth," screw, two decker, 91 guns. Flagship of Admiral Michael Seymour, ...	W. K. Hall.
"Nile," screw, two decker, 91 guns, ...	Mundy.
"Cæsar," ,, ,, ,, ...	Robb.
"Orion," ,, ,, ,, ...	Erskine.

C

				CAPTAINS.
"James Watt," screw, two decker,		91 guns,	...	Elliot.
"Powerful," sailing,	,,	84 guns,	...	Massie.
"Calcutta," ,,	,,	,,	...	Stopford.
"Cressy," screw,	,,	80 guns,	...	Warren.
"Majestic," ,,	,,	,,	...	Hope.
"Colossus," ,,	,,	,,	...	Robinson.
"Sanspariel," ,,	,,	70 guns,	...	Williams.
"Edinburgh," ,,	blockship,	60 guns,	...	Hewlett.
"Hogue," ,,	,,	,,	...	Ramsay.
"Ajax," ,,	,,	,,	...	Warden.
"Blenheim," ,,	,,	,,		W. H. Hall.
"Odin," paddle,		16 guns,	...	Wilcox.
"Vulture," ,,		6 guns,	...	Glass.

In addition to the above, there were also a large number of gun and mortar boats in various stages of preparation for active service. From the foregoing, the sailing vessels, which were not to go to the Baltic, must be deducted; but, on the other hand, the steam fleet was to be augmented from other ports to 20 screw line of battle ships, besides frigates, corvettes, paddles, gun and mortar vessels, bringing up a total of 100 sail of all classes. The British Baltic Fleet thus to be constituted was, in numbers and armament, far beyond any Nelson ever had under his command. The "Duke" alone, I recorded with pride, could discharge a ton and a half of metal at each broadside; while the united broadsides of the Spithead fleet numbered six hundred shot. These statistics at the time looked overwhelming; yet, how small compared with the weight of metal of our latter day ironclads!

The united crews of the Baltic Fleet of 1855 mustered about 24,000 men, (always exclusive of the French) of which 3,000 were marines, armed with the Minie Rifle. The latter would be an efficient infantry force in the event of a landing, and also the sharp shooters of their respective ships. The "Duke" alone carried 194, and each two decker about 150 marines. If the *personnel* of the Allied Fleets thus ran into heavy totals, it must be remembered that, in numbers, the Russians were also truly formidable.

This day the fleet was inspected by the Lords of the Admiralty, who cruised round in the "Black Eagle," and finally came on board the "Duke." They were Sir Charles Wood, (civil lord), and Admirals Sir Baldwin Walker, Berkeley, and Eden, naval lords.

On Wednesday, the 4th, the ship was astir at an unusually early hour, from which the knowing ones judged something was coming; and, true enough, in the forenoon up went the long expected signal for the fleet to weigh and sail.

The scene of bustle and excitement which followed can hardly be described. The morning was gloomy, but gradually brightened, and soon the water was absolutely covered with pleasure steamers, and every conceivable kind of craft, crowded with thousands of sightseers. The "Victory" boomed a gun every five minutes; bands played, men cheered, women waved handkerchiefs, and everyone offered good luck to the noble fleet. The Port Admiral, Sir Thomas Cochrane, a most venerable veteran, whose service ran back to the days of Nelson, steamed through the fleet, flying a signal "good-bye and good luck." It was indeed a scene to move the most stolid. I watched our anchor being weighed, as a host of excited sailors and marines spun round the capstan with steady tramp, to the lively "Lea Rig," or the "Girl I left behind me," played by the band. How different from the dreadful work of the modern horrid "donkey engine." There is some sentiment in muscular manhood—none in mere mechanics! At last, by 3 p.m., the great Fleet was under weigh, with easy steam and sail, to rendezvous in the Downs.

The Spithead forts saluted as we passed, and a few shells playfully thrown in the air burst very beautifully. Outside the Isle of Wight three lines were formed, of which the "Duke," under easy steam, led the port or inner squadron.

Tired out by the day's doings we nearly all turned in early, and about 9.30 I got into my hammock, somewhat in doubt as to the nature of my slumbers, with a rumbling screw not far from my head. Before my doubts could be resolved, the whole ship was rudely aroused by an unexpected catastrophe; first came a shock, and a quiver from stem to stern; then a crashing, tearing noise overhead, mingled with frantic yells of "stop her, stop her."

In an instant every one was on his feet, in night shirts simply, or half dressed. The words rapidly passed—"we're aground," "we're rundown"; but speedily the true explanation transpired—"we've been in collision." I hastened to my rallying place—the sick bay—but found no need for me there, as no one seemed injured. On reaching the quarter deck, the nature of the accident was soon revealed. Although it was fair moonlight, a full-rigged ship, without lights or look-out, came right down upon us, driving an anchor into our bows, tearing off the port bulwarks and hammock netting, and carrying away part of the mainyard. As a souvenir, she left pieces of her head gear and foremast on our deck.

Our damage, although extensive, was not

immediately crippling, but there was much speculation how it fared with our assailant, who had disappeared astern. We fired a gun, and sent a steamer to look for her.

After this we went ahead as if nothing had happened, and presently were snug again among our respective blankets.

But when day-light came, the damage to the "Duke" proved to be such as would necessitate her return to Spithead for repairs. I will draw a veil over the language used towards the unknown ship when this became known! Although some of our men had narrow escapes in the collision, no one was seriously injured, and only a few slightly bruised.

During the forenoon of the 5th we passed Dover, amid a great ovation from crowds on the white cliffs ; and, shortly afterwards, "All in the Downs the Fleet was moored." Crowds of both sexes soon visited us, but I failed to identify the charming "Black Eyed Susan," or the ideal "Sweet William." The 6th being Good Friday we rode quietly at anchor; on the 7th the Admiral shifted his flag to the "Nile," and at noon, to our infinite disgust, we left the Downs alone for Spithead for repairs. We arrived there on Sunday morning, the 8th, and anchored quietly at the spot from which we had recently so gaily started. Hardly was the anchor down when we were boarded by a gang of shipwrights, who forthwith set about the repairs.

We learned that the ship which had so grossly fouled us was a big Yankee, bound from Antwerp to New York, with 300 German emigrants, who had meanwhile been transferred to a hulk while she was being repaired. Her skipper had been spinning wonderful yarns all over Portsmouth, to shield himself, but was aghast when he heard a Court of inquiry was to sit on the "Victory." When ordered to attend he refused, and tried to bounce; but quietly condescended to appear and explain matters, when he found the Britisher meant business, and would stand no nonsense. It is needless to say the entire blame of the collision was found to rest with this careless and contumacious dog, who richly deserved a rope end.

Being in the hands of the shipwrights, we were given to understand we could have unlimited shore leave, of which we were not slow to avail ourselves.

CHAPTER IV.

LIFE ON THE "DUKE."

MY first shore visit, on the 9th, was spent in the Dockyard. then the scene of extraordinary activity, no less than 3000 men being on day and night shifts, chiefly employed on the much wanted gun and mortar boats. The extent and resources of the Dockyard greatly impressed me. The "Marlborough," sister ship to the "Duke," and pierced for 131 guns, was then well advanced on the stocks; but although launched in due time, this magnificent vessel never was commissioned, having had the misfortune, through the advent of ironclads. in 1859, in the French " La Gloire," to become prematurely obsolete.

On returning to the "Duke" in the evening, with several messmates, in the boat of a well known waterman. named Long, it was so rough and stormy that Duncan begged him to put back; but the old salt—already three sheets in the wind —only said, "She'll go like a duck;" and she did—giving us a thorough drenching.

During a week of inactivity. I embraced the opportunity of taking stock of my ship and shipmates. A lover of ships and sailors, I was immensely proud of the superb vessel to which I belonged ; never weary in contemplating, investigating, and admiring her noble decks, fittings, and batteries; and never tired in noting the splendid physique and temper of officers, sailors and marines. I recognised in their thoroughness and heartiness the true secret of British discipline and power. My conclusion was, and still is : the typical English man o' war's man is essentially *sui generis*—a man unmatched in the whole world ; those of foreign navies seem but indifferent imitations of him ; he alone is the genuine article—a true sailor. Foreign naval seamen too often convey the impression of conscripted landsmen masquerading in nautical disguise.

The noble " Duke" was not only the largest and finest three decker afloat, or as yet had sailed the seas, but was so complete and up to date at the time, that, had any one hinted she would be really obsolete in less than a decade, he would have been laughed to scorn ! Yet, such proved the fact : in less than ten years the poetic and glorious wooden walls of old England were being supplanted by prosaic ugly iron monsters like the " Warrior " and " Black Prince !"

The " Duke " originally was laid down as the sailing " Windsor Castle," but her construction was delayed by the introduction of the screw propeller, which caused her to be lengthened and fitted for steam. The change in her name was consequent on the death of the great Duke of Wellington in 1852. Thus transformed, in substance and in name, she was commissioned with an armament of 131 guns, and a crew of 1200 officers and men of all grades. Her dimensions were as follows:—length 270, beam 60, depth 60, draught 27—increased in the semi-fresh waters of the

THE "DUKE."

Baltic to 29 feet; tonnage 3,700; engine power 780 horse.

She had three fighting decks from six to seven feet in height; the lower and middle decks were armed with hollow 56 and solid 32 pounders; the upper deck with 32 pounders; and the quarter-deck with brass guns. The odd gun was a great swivel solid 68 pounder, mounted on traversing rails on the forecastle. The cockpit deck was partly under the water line; the magazines and engines wholly so. Between the rows of cannon on the fighting decks iron rances supported six rounds of black shining shot for each gun; the overhead beam racks held the rammers and sponges of the guns, and also the short muskets and cutlasses of the sailors. At intervals on the decks were stands for the long rifles of the marines.

The magnificently kept decks and armament were always a sight to see; but particularly interesting when the mess tables were down, and spread with a substantial repast, at which hundreds of hearty fellows partook.

At night the lower deck, on which were slung 800 hammocks, was a curious sight. The hammocks, bulging with the sleepers, were like herrings in a barrel, and it was a break back business walking under them. If, by accident, the stooper bumped against one, the chances were the expletives evoked were more forcible than polite!

Aft of the quarter deck were the cabins of the Admiral, Captain, and Staff.

Aft of the middle deck, the Ward Room of the senior officers.

Aft of the lower deck, the Gun Room for the junior officers.

These apartments, however, were merely railed off from the fighting decks by moveable bulkheads, which were cleared away at general quarters. The senior officers had fixed cabins in the cockpit.

There was, of course, more stately dignity in the Ward than the Gun Room; but at my then time of life, I much preferred the free and easy fun and frolic of the latter.

The Gun Room of the "Duke" was much the largest in the Fleet, and would have been reckoned a magnificent Ward Room in Trafalgar days. It measured 40 feet by 20, with a great mahogany table athwart ships, flanked by very strong chairs, fitted to meet the rough usage to which they were often subjected. It was absolutely undecorated, beyond engravings of the Queen and Prince Albert; and two prints of nameless female faces, just, in their loveliness, to keep us in mind of those we had left behind.

As we juniors had no cabins, the Gun Room was our sole apartment for all purposes; consequently, in domestic language, it was often, if not generally, very untidy. Among other things it was the school room of the naval instructor, Mr Onslow, and as such was daily strewn with the writing desks, nautical books, dictionaries — aye, and cheap novels of the young "middy" scholars. For, as boys will be boys, all the show of nautical learning did not indicate much; and study was decidedly less popular than fencing, sparring, wrestling, and general sky-larking. Parallel with the bulkheads, the steward, Mr Whitcomb, had a bunk, in which that stout, butler-looking man, with his myrmidons, stowed and well guarded the stock of wines, spirits, jams, and other delicacies, which were supplied under strict sumptuary regulations. As an unfinished pot or bottle was labelled with the owner's name, and taken in charge by the steward until again wanted, it is needless to say there must have been very considerable pickings from the broken delicacies of some thirty none too exacting members of the mess. But I never heard the steward accused of malversation, and, indeed, he had no occasion to be mean, having almost unlimited supplies to draw upon. The daily free ship ration of each officer, consisted of meat, bread, potatoes, pepper, salt, mustard, tea, coffee, cocoa, sugar, flour, suet, currants, &c., according to alternate issues, all of which went in bulk into the mess: and butcher meat, fowls, hams, fish, butter, eggs, &c., were also purchased as required. We thus fed like fighting cocks, at a money cost per head per diem of about one shilling!

Wines and spirits were obtained, duty free, on extra payment. The cost of messing was therefore most moderate. Officers of a certain seniority also drew a free ration of rum, but midshipmen were not included, some of whom were big strapping fellows; they were also forbidden to purchase spirits, and even limited in an allowance of port and sherry from the Steward's stores. But the notorious futility of sumptuary regulations was illustrated even here; for many a time I stood a wheedling youngster a glass of grog from my bottle; and even swapped my rum ration for a week on end with a friendly middy for pots of jam! Did any one ever notice the young gentlemen drinking grog? Of course not!

The joyous, frolicsome spirit which pervaded our mess was naturally carried to the cockpit, which, if somewhat dismal at hammock time, was often the scene of much rough and tumble fun. Where not taken up by sea chests, this deck was lumbered with a variety of stores. having one thing in common—a tarry smell. Over and around such piles the youngsters often carried on high jinks—such as a battle royal with hammock pillows—until the Master at Arms (a Discipline Warrant Officer) would put in an appearance, with a shout, " Now, then, gentlemen, turn in at once," an order always promptly obeyed. All such cruel jokes, as cutting down hammocks, were discouraged, and the larking, if noisy, was generally quite harmless. When watching these little games from my hammock, I have seen my nearest neighbour—a meek and pious acting Assistant Surgeon—on his knees, by his chest, saying his prayers. Although unmolested, he did not seem to realize the needless incongruity of the situation.

CHAPTER V.

ROUTINE OF A WAR SHIP.

ON Wednesday the 11th the entry in my diary is headed—"Routine of a War Ship," in which I repeat much often told before, but which can yet stand re-telling ; and also observe it were well to get over yarns about ship and shipmates before reaching the Baltic, where it was to be hoped more exciting subjects would engage attention. There was plenty of time for observation, for my duties were far from onerous, and with a healthy crew there was but little for the five or six medical officers to do. The sick bay was visited at 7 a.m., 1 p.m., and 5 p.m., with, of course, casual calls as required. Time was, of course, not reckoned by the clock, but by the number of bells struck in a given watch. Within the twenty-four hours, there are nominally six watches of four hours each, but in reality actually seven, as that between 4 and 8 p.m. is divided into two, called " dog watches," through which the ship's company reliefs are enabled to change watches, and thus secure variety in the time and turn of duty. A four hour watch is divided by bells struck every half hour ; thus, say half-past twelve—one bell ; one o'clock—two bells; and so on to eight bells; then relief, and *da capo.*

The morning watch at sea begins at eight bells of the first watch, or four a.m.; in harbour at two bells of the second watch, or five a.m. No sooner are these bells struck than the piping of the boatswain's is heard; followed by stentorian shouts of "Turn out"; this is instantly obeyed, without any preliminary period of yawning or eye opening. The hammocks are at once laced up, with the bedding inside, unslung, and carried to the quarterdeck for stowage in the hammock netting on the bulwarks.

The officers meanwhile have an hour's grace, but must then turn out with equal promptness, and be in uniform by six or seven o'clock as the case may be.

The Steward's store is at once thrown open, and representatives from each mess proceed with bags to draw the daily allowance of biscuits. About an hour after the turn out, another series of whistlings and yellings begin, with the order "Clean decks"; and immediately a confused sound of scouring, scraping, rubbing, swabbing, commences, with a constant swish swash of water from buckets and hose, until the decks are as clean as a model housewife's kitchen table. The wayfarer on the decks, be he officer or man, at the time of cleaning must take his chance of splashing, for no respect of persons is then shown, and nothing allowed to hinder the work.

At eight bells second watch—8 a.m.—comes the welcome announcement of "breakfast ready"; at two bells—9 a.m.—the marine drummers indulge in a rub-a-dub call for "divisions," at which all the fighting men muster with arms in hand for inspection and roll call. Woe to the wretch who presents himself or his arms dirty or untidy! During divisions the band plays on the quarter-deck, and the officers not on duty promenade, until the whole is over by four bells — 10 o'clock. The next event of moment is eight bells —12 o'clock—when the men and Gun Room officers have dinner, while the denizens of the Ward Room have luncheon. At two bells, or 5 o'clock of the dog watch, there are short quarters or divisions parade, and at four bells—6 o'clock—the men and Gun Room officers have tea, while the Ward Room officers dine to the strains of the band. The latter plays till eight bells—eight o'clock—or by permission an hour longer, when officers and men perhaps indulge in a dance. But at eight bells the hammocks are piped down, and by two bells—9 o'clock—the most of the ship's company have turned in, while the officers must follow suit at four bells—10 o'clock—unless granted special permission to be up. At the latter hour the Captain or the Commander, accompanied by certain officers and warrant officers on duty, begins a ghostly round of the whole ship, with lanterns, to see that everything is right and tight for the night.

The decks of a man-of-war at the time I describe, were lit at night with huge reflecting oil lamps, in the dim light of which duty was as strictly carried out as in the blaze of day. I remember, when awake one night, watching the marine sentry in the cockpit being relieved, and noticing that the presenting of arms, and all other formalities, were carried out in the semi-darkness with complete precision, at which I wondered; for I had not then learned the lesson that inflexible

routine between individuals on duty, and the
minute carrying out of detail, constitutes the very
essence and foundation of discipline in a fighting
force—whether on land or sea. The British army
and navy are what they are through their steady
sense of duty, and absence of mere eye-service.

The foregoing constitutes the ordinary routine
of daily duty on a warship; but it is needless to
remark that there are an immense number of other
duties and drills, which it is impossible to specify.
To keep such a huge machine as a line of battle
ship in trim requires an amount and continuity of
labour scarcely to be realised.

The drill alone needed to fit all on board for
their specific individual duties must be incessantly
practised. Take "general" and "fire" quarters.
General quarters mean when the decks are cleared
and made ready for action, and every officer and
man stands by his allotted work; fire quarters,
when the hose is run out, buckets got ready, provision made for flooding the magazines, for lowering boats, &c., as if the ship were on fire.

Ordinary drill, of which due notice is given,
presents no unusual features; but it is otherwise
when these quarters are summoned, without
any warning, perhaps in the middle of the night.
This we felt in the Baltic while in front of the
enemy, when no one knew whether the occasional
sudden sounding of general quarters was a sham or
a reality. The fire bell in the middle of the night
sounds uncommonly weird and alarming. The
rudely awakened sleeper cannot for a time grasp
whether the ship may not actually be on fire; but
alarm is speedily dispelled by the sense of security
which the assurance of united action and discipline
imparts.

But it must not be supposed that life on board a great man o' war is one eternal and monotonous round of duty and drill. There is much leisure, and all sorts of games and amusements practised to kill time, and lighten existence. In every ship and mess kindly chance always supplies a certain number of cheery and sometimes eccentric individuals, whose function it is to keep things moving. In such a great community as the crew of the "Duke," all sorts of individual character were to be found; hence, to study the idiosyncrasies of one's shipmates was a diverting recreation for those so inclined. To this object I shall devote the next chapter.

D

CHAPTER VI.

SHIPMATES.

AMONG our sailors and marines were many splendid specimens of the *genus homo ;* and it is a proud consolation to know that, in these latter days, not only is there no deterioration in the physique of our navy men, but some say it is even finer than ever. The training of men from boyhood is the means by which this is attained. But the type of our sailors naturally changes and varies with the times, and the man of the ironclad is unquestionably different from his wooden wall predecessor. Among the petty officers and A.B.'s of the Baltic Fleet we had many tars, clean-shaven, with long locks curled and oiled, just as in Nelson's days—barring the pigtails. These were men essentially of the type of which Dibdin sang—the Ben Bobstay's, and Jack Rackstraw's of renown. But among the ordinary seamen we had many merchant sailors, or pure landsmen, who, in several respects, still lacked the true characteristics of navy men. Yet, it was astonishing how soon, under strict discipline, they were licked into the normal shape. The Marine Artillery, who worked the pivot forecastle gun, were men of selected strength and stature. The Infantry Marine was in every sense a model soldier. Of the entire crew, sailors and marines, it may be said the leading characteristic was unfailing give and take good humour. Its great value was seen in the avoidance of quarrels, and the general sweetening of the collective life. How much would civic, and even domestic life, be improved if this principle was similarly and equally honourably carried out?

Music on board was largely cultivated. Each mess had its singers, and fairly good fiddlers were numerous. Dancing was a fine art, and had many very capable exponents.

Among the officers, variety in appearance and character was so conspicuous as to afford me a fruitful field for speculation. After forty years I can now speak of these excellent gentlemen in terms which at the time would have been rank impertinence. The seniors I knew less of, yet, with eyes and ears open, I could form a very fair estimate of them from a distance. The juniors were, so to speak, at command; for nowhere as on shipboard are the strength and weaknesses of comrades more apparent.

First came the Admiral in supreme command. The Honourable Richard Saunders Dundas—afterwards K.C.B.—just turned 50, and reckoned young for the position, having considerable influence through being a younger brother of Lord Melville. He was a handsome Scotsman, spare and upright, features clean cut, with regulation mutton-chop whiskers; a very quiet well mannered gentleman, and if a strict, a kindly disciplinarian; in these respects somewhat of a contrast to his predecessor of 1854, bluff, old Sir Charles Napier. I never heard Dundas accused of a rough or unkind word or action.

Next was Commodore, the Honourable Frederick Pelham, on the Admiral's staff, a most gallant and corteous sailor, whom we all loved. Personally, he was a lean, bald-headed, pantaloon-like man, with a cast in one eye. He was called the hero of Bomarsund, from his gallantry at the capture of that fort in 1854.

The Captain, Henry Caldwell, was reckoned one of the handsomest and best officers in the navy; an exceedingly good-looking open-faced man, turned forty, of powerful physique, and with a voice like a trumpet. It was something to hear him drilling the men aloft in stentorian shouts. Although, officially, very stand off and dignified, yet it was not difficult to discover he was socially frank and kind hearted.

Commander George W. Preedy was a sturdy, round bodied, red faced man, full of energy; a splendid seaman, and thorough disciplinarian, but in private a most kindly and considerate man. He died in 1894.

Among the Lieutenants were some fine fellows. The senior, Hannen, between thirty and forty years of age, seemed somehow to have missed promotion; and never got it; for, although his gaunt face was deeply pitted with small-pox, he died, strange to say, of a second attack of the disease in the Baltic.

He was succeeded by the Honourable Augustus Hobart, destined to be afterwards known world-wide as Hobart Pasha, commanding the Turkish Navy. All round he was as perfect an ideal British naval officer as one could picture: not too tall, but broad and powerful, a manly voice, and a face frank and open as the noon day: a born leader of men, as afterwards proved.

Lieutenant, now Admiral, Thomas Barnardiston was a dapper, very reserved, little man, credited by his fellows with being a very good officer.

Lieutenant W. E., now Admiral, Gordon was a Scotsman of much amiability, with a thin, fair face always radiant with good humour.

Lieutenant J. K. Baird—familiarly "Jock"—was a tall, powerful, dare-devil Scotsman, a lineal and typical descendant of "Oor Davie," the famous Sir David Baird of Seringapatam. He was the sort of man nothing could stop or daunt, and lived to be Admiral Sir John Baird, commanding the Channel Fleet in 1888.

The First Master was Henry Moriarty, a very quiet man, who, cat-like, glided noiselessly about, and spoke little; but the fact of his appointment to the "Duke" stamped him a first-rate navigator.

There were three Surgeons, and at various times four Assistant Surgeons on board, besides More and myself. The senior Surgeon, Le Grand, was an old and rather worn-out officer, who, on arrival in the Baltic, was speedily invalided for bronchitis. After him, Surgeons Domville and Jeffcoat were appointed, than between whom it were scarcely possible to imagine a greater contrast. The first was tall, thin, cold, and dignified; the second, short, flabby, snuffy, and garrulous. More likened the former to a wax taper, and the latter to a mere tallow dip!

Assistant Surgeon George Duncan was a hearty, red whiskered, bluff, and somewhat peppery Scot; but a most sincere, kindly fellow. He died in 1889.

George Banks, another Assistant Surgeon, was a tall, dandy, and rather lady-killing man. He has been dead for a number of years.

The Chaplain and Naval Instructor, the Rev. A. Onslow, was a high bred, learned Oxford graduate — a typical English clergyman, who commanded complete respect. On retirement from the Navy he was in such high repute as to be presented by the Prince of Wales to the living of Sandringham, where he died.

Lieutenant-Colonel Joseph Oates Travers, who commanded the Royal Marines, was a very striking person, immensely tall, square, and thin, and of a knightly, soldierly bearing. He at once and irresistibly recalled an ideal Don Quixote.

Captain Nugent, who was consulting Royal Engineer on board, was then a very good-looking young man. Fifteen years later, as Colonel Nugent, he was my commanding officer in Bermuda; and after the lapse of another similar period, as Sir Charles Nugent, my friend in the War Office.

The Interpreter was Mr Hill, an Englishman of magnificent physique, who, having been partly brought up in St Petersburgh, could speak Russian, Finnish, French, and German as fluently as English.

All the foregoing were Ward Room officers; and the last I shall mention was my own particular and good friend, Paymaster Richard Munday, who was the Admiral's secretary. Tall, good-looking, blue-eyed, he was a thorough Englishman, frank and sincere, of good education, and high ability. To him I am indebted for a great deal recorded in these reminiscences. He was ever ready to impart all and every detail, new to me, regarding naval life; and, as he could trust me, I got much information from him, which at the time was in many ways, and for obvious reasons, confidential, although long ago public property. I am glad to think he still lives in honoured retirement in Devonshire, and can only live in hope of some day meeting him once more.

My friends in the Gun Room were, of course, familiar to me in a much closer way than those in the Ward Room.

The senior in years, among a crowd of comparative youngsters, was Assistant Paymaster Robert Bone, a man of perhaps six and twenty; a spruce, red-whiskered Devonian, who never tired extolling what he called the "west country." His stock song was "The Pope." I met him once afterwards in Bermuda, returning home in broken health, from which he did not long survive.

The First Mate (for that good old fashioned title was then extant), Parker, met my ideal of a typical British tar of the olden school; square, strong, active as a cat, he was just the man to head a boarding party cutlass in hand. His hairless, weather-beaten face, and pensive blue eye, gave him, at twenty, the look of thirty.

The Senior Midshipman, although barely twenty, also looked thirty. From his fancied resemblance to "Mr Pickwick"—fat podgy body, red face, and croaky voice—he bore the nick-name of "Picky." In truth, he both ate and drank too much; and in these respects had crowded into his hobble-de-hoy-hood the experiences of a blasé man.

Middy Fawkes ("Guy," of course,) was the comedian of the mess, and a very droll fellow. Although of an old Yorkshire family, his strange parrot nose, and black eyes, gave him a decided Hebraic look. He sang, or rather shouted, for he had no melody, a variety of nautical ditties with fearful vigour; but the hearty good humour he threw into his vocal efforts always evoked much applause. His name long since disappeared from the Navy List, and I never heard what became of him.

Middy Eden, a remarkably handsome lad, of a distinguished naval family, was one of my special friends. His youth and junior rank precluded him from the "grog ration," but many is the time he had mine. As a souvenir, he presented me with a Russian short sword, which he had taken from the body of a dead Artilleryman at the capture of Bomarsund, and which I carefully retain until this day. What ultimately became of this fine young fellow, as well as many others of the mess, I do not know.

The smallest soul on board was Cadet Lockhart, a Scot of twelve years, and even diminutive for his age. Some of the bigger of us used to tuck him under an arm and run off with him. It was comical to watch this mite giving orders to burly tars, who obeyed with a forelock salute, and "aye, aye, sir."

My friend and colleague, More, was, of course, a companion with whom I spent many an hour. The son of a Fife minister, he was a man of liberal education, and highly philosophical mind. He settled in Rothwell, Northampton, where he still lives; and although in busy private practice found time to write various essays on psychological subjects.

Besides the ship's own officers, the "Duke," as flagship, carried a number of supernumeraries, who were constantly coming and going in the Fleet. One of these was a clerk named Potts, a perfect curiosity; a thorough Cockney, he had

lived much on the Continent, and spoke French
and German with the utmost fluency ; indeed he
was as much Parisian as Londoner. Although
only about five and twenty, he had a shrunken
body, and wizened face, which, with lank, red hair
combed back, gave him a foreign appearance.
His extraordinary vivacity and decided talents,
however, made him an agreeable companion, and a
jolly messmate. There were also two other
Cockney clerks, who, having none of the liveliness
of Potts, were, I am afraid, the very butts of the
mess, and were subjected to every species of
ludicrous sport and trick. Lastly, there was a
clerk named Crowe ("Jim," of course), whose
father was Consul at Christiania, where he had
been brought up. "Jim's" fleshy body, towy
hair, light blue eye, and broken speech, proclaimed
him more a Scandanavian than Englishman. He
was the subject of many pleasantries, but his
simplicity and unfailing good temper made him a
great favourite.

And where, after the passage of four decades,
are all these young fellows now, then, so sprightly
and hopeful, on the threshold of manhood? Alas!
alas! probably not a third are left to recount a
forty years' battle ; and even of that remnant,
how many have been successful in the fight!

CHAPTER VII.

RENDEZVOUS AT KIEL.

AT last the continued hammering of the shipwrights ceased, and our repairs were completed. On Monday, 16th April, we slipped quietly away, very differently from "the pomp and circumstance" which marked our first departure.

We witnessed a glorious red sunset in passing up the Channel, which proved the precursor of dirty head weather from the east, and necessitated getting up steam. On the morning of the 17th we fell in with the Channel Fleet, which had been escorting and saluting the French Emperor and Empress on their memorable visit to the Queen; and arrived in the Downs about midnight, in heavy weather, which caused 140 fathoms of our gigantic chain cable to run out before the ship was brought to anchor. As each link of the cable weighed 30 lbs., and 7 links went to the fathom, this meant the running out of about 14 tons weight of chain iron!

In the Downs we encountered the French Squadron, which had accompanied the Emperor, of which the finest vessel was the two decker, "Austerlitz," 100 guns, having for a figure-head a splendid effigy of Napoleon I., and three large gilt eagles on the stern. The *Entente Cordial* was then in full swing, destined in less than three years to reaction over Orsini's doings in 1858; and to extinction in 1859 over the cock-a-doodle-doing of the French "Colonels;" which, moreover, was the initial cause of our great Volunteer movement. So it has ever been in the history of transient fraternity between unkindred races and nations.

The signal was flown on the 18th to join the Fleet at Kiel, and we sailed alone. The shortening of the enormously run out cable was a long job, and an exhilarating sight, with no less than 180 men spinning round the capstan to the strains of the band.

By 3 p.m. the last outline of the English coast disappeared, while we sang together, in the Gun Room, "Isle of Beauty, fare thee well." All were indeed moved by the thought that we were now fairly off on war service; but we were merrier than usual, so that even the taciturn Cockney clerk, Fesenmayer, volunteered a recitation, which sent us into fits! Next day we passed within a few miles of the scene of the memorable battle of Camperdown—steaming through crowds of Dutch luggers and fishing boats. On the 20th we had a taste of general quarters, in rough, cold weather, which brought those to book who had not yet got their sea legs. The following day we knocked about under double reefed topsails, fully realizing what a North Sea gale is in the latitude between Scotland and Denmark. It was my first experience of sea sickness, and, with many of my comrades, I was glad to turn into a hammock early in the evening. When the gale abated on Sunday, 22nd, we were within easy reach of the Shetlands instead of our objective—the Naze of Norway, which we did not sight until the 23rd.

On the same day our first death occurred, in the

person of a seaman named William Hall, who died of apoplexy; his was the first funeral at sea I had witnessed; the body was stitched up in an old hammock, with a 32 pound shot at the feet; the crew assembled on middle deck to the slow tolling of the ship's bell; a gun was run back, and a port opened; in reverent silence the chaplain read the burial service at sea; and, at a given signal, the corpse was slipped overboard, plunging with a splash to its last resting place, "full many a fathom deep."

On the 24th, in beautiful weather, we entered the Cattegat, and steamed down the Great Belt next day, between the pretty Danish islands. A pilot came on board at Nyborg, as the navigation was difficult, in water so shallow that every revolution of the screw brought up mud. In passing Funen and Langland, we could almost have hailed the peasant folks, busy at their spring sowing, who in turn gazed at us in mute astonishment. About 10 p.m., we anchored 12 miles from Kiel, towards which we moved off next morning about 5 o'clock.

The prospect on entering the spacious firth was very pretty and homely; ploughs were busy on the braes, and farm labour going on; the fisher folks were all astir—some propelling tiny skiffs with sculls like corn scoops; others in larger boats towing perforated boxes full of live fish for the Fleet. At 8 a.m. we saluted our comrades, from whom we had so unwillingly been separated, and once more anchored as the rightful Flagship. The Admiral, however, was away in Copenhagen, and did not immediately join us. Being a show ship we were speedily inundated by shoals of visitors. Keil, a fine old town of 20,000 inhabitants, was then the capital of Danish Schleswig-Holstien, and no one dreamt that in another decade it would be the chief port of the German Navy. The harbour is land-locked and spacious, affording anchorage for a large Fleet. Here we lay for five days, and received numerous sight-seers all the way from Hamburg and Berlin. Two deaths occurred during our stay—a fireman killed by falling into the stoke hole; and a marine, from what was considered malignant measles, but which, we afterwards believed to be undeveloped small-pox; both were buried on shore. On our first visit to the town we landed at Bellvue, and had a walk of a mile, by a road between trim trees and hedge-rows: it was crowded with people going towards the Fleet, who, with much politeness, saluted our uniform. The polyglot Potts was our German interpreter—a language generally understood, although little spoken. As far as the general appearance of the people was concerned, I could have imagined myself among my countrymen in the north-east of Scotland—both being unquestionably of the self-same stock. The men smoked, and nearly all wore beards and moustachoes, which had not then been adopted at home, and gave them a foreign appearance which would not be observable now-a-days. They were simple, kindly folks, and without introduction, several of us were invited to tea in a private house, where conversation was carried on chiefly by signs. It was impossible not to be struck by the simplicity, homeliness, and unconventionality of the people. We attended a ball, or weekly hop, where everybody, in morning dress, seemed to dance with anybody, without formality or introduction.

The streets of Kiel looked primitive, even compared with an old English town; for they were still lit by oil lamps suspended from cross ropes. The houses were gay in colour, light in contour, and literally stuck full of windows.

Having been joined by the Admiral and his Staff, and restored to our position as Flagship, we weighed anchor on Thursday, May 3rd, for Faro Sound, at the north extremity of the Swedish island of Gothland.

When the firth was cleared the Fleet formed in two divisions, the starboard led by the "Duke," and the port by the "Exmouth," the latter carrying the pennant of Admiral Seymour.

We were met by the "Conflict" bearing despatches from the Flying Squadron, which for some weeks had been watching the breaking up of the ice in the Gulf of Finland.

On the 4th we had general quarters, with, for the first time, firing of blank cartridge. The noise overhead was something terrific, and in a short time we were nearly suffocated by sulphureous fumes at our stations in the cockpit. One could then realise the awful nature of a general naval action.

In the evening we passed the rocky, but well wooded island of Bornholm, still with patches of snow on the heights.

On the morning of the 5th we sighted Utklipporna lighthouse on the Swedish mainland; and in the evening Hoborg light on South Gothland.

Early on the morning of the 6th we arrived and anchored in the shallow waters of Faro Sound, about a mile and a half from the shore.

Here, to our alarm and disgust, we found the "Arrogant," 44 guns, of the Flying Squadron.

with small-pox on board, and forming an hospital at Faro for the reception and isolation of the cases.

What little we could see of Faro was most uninviting. It is a low island separated from north Gothland by a narrow channel. We were soon surrounded by bum boats, with fowls, fish, milk, butter, and eggs, and even sheep and bullocks for sale. A few intensely rustic and Scandanavian women came on board, and in the most comic way drew from beneath the folds of their ample petticoats the live fowls they wished to dispose of. Some of the lusty dames could speak a few words of English, which they had picked up from contact with the ubiquitous British sailor.

On the 7th a collier came alongside to discharge, and I was agreeably surprised to find her the "Brittania" of Arbroath, commanded by my friend Captain David Cargill. I speedily got him on board, and took him all round the "Duke," with whose size and armament he was deeply impressed. Over a convivial glass in the Gun Room he assured us he knew Cronstadt well, and we had nothing to do but steam between the forts and blow them out of the water! Our Admiral, however, took a different view of such a method of attack from our valiant skipper. On leaving for his own craft, David said: "Why, I could step from your quarter deck on to my maintop!"

On the 8th, the Fleet left Faro, steering east, for a secret rendezvous; some thought it would be Riga, and some Revel; but when we sighted Dago our destination was clearly Revel. We had to steam cautiously on an east north-east course, being now on the enemy's seaboard, with every light and beacon carefully extinguished or removed. Presently we entered the Gulf of

Finland, but not a sail was visible any more than in the open ocean; for the Russians had a wholesome dread of our cruisers of the Flying Squadron, which had been scouring about.

As we made easting, the temperature fell decidedly, but all ice had disappeared. It was very cold for May, although the weather was fine.

We slowly felt our way up the Gulf, and, at 4 a.m. on the morning of the 10th, anchored about a mile off the east of the island of Nargen, which was completely under our command; and about four miles from the frowning batteries of Revel, which, after Cronstadt and Sweaborg, is the largest naval fortress of the Russians in the Baltic.

CHAPTER VIII.

REVEL AND NARGEN.

MY first thoughts on waking up were—we are almost within gunshot of an enemy's fortress, and the Baltic Fleet is now vindicating its name and function in sealing up hostile squadrons, and so letting the good folks of our maritime towns at home rest in security. Such a reflection was neither idle nor inappropriate, but was it sufficiently appreciated? On returning home, I was asked, by a narrow and captious Radical in Aberdeen, what good the Baltic Fleet had done? to which I replied, with natural warmth and contempt: "Why, enabled your unthankful head to sleep in peace; and probably kept your blessed house from being knocked about your ears." The "friend of every country but his own" made no reply.

I turned out very early, and on reaching the quarterdeck proceeded to take in as much as possible of our surroundings, especially of the island of which we were the temporary masters, and the fortress of which we much desired to be.

Nargen is low and sandy, 9 miles in length, by from 1 to 2 in breadth; it is almost covered with pine woods, and has a scanty Finnish, or Swedish, fishing population, whom we were cautioned not to molest; it lies off the Ethonian shore, about four or five miles from Revel; it was as we found—an old rendezvous for a British Fleet. An armed party at once proceeded on shore to scour the island, and establish an outlook from the dismantled light-house.

Revel lay due south, and with a glass was plainly visible; for the atmosphere in the Baltic in the summer months is remarkably transparent. Every fort and prominent object could be clearly identified, of which the most conspicuous was the Domberg, or Cathedral, on a precipitous height; and on another height the High Church. Between these heights is the seaward approach to the town, which then contained about 30,000 inhabitants. The batteries commanding the roadstead were partly earth and partly granite; and of the latter one was a huge casemated fort of 300 guns. From it the smoke of furnaces for heating red hot shot was constantly visible. At our standpoint Revel was singularly pretty.

On the day after arrival targets were placed out for practice for our own benefit, and probably to waken up the enemy. The accuracy of the firing greatly pleased me, as the slender flagstaffs on floating barrels were constantly being shot down. The whole proceeding was keenly watched from Revel.

The 12th being a general holiday we proceeded *en masse* on shore, and I put my first foot on Russian soil. We ran our boat on the beach, beside a number of native fishing craft. We made straight for the village, which was a mere motley aggregation of cabins, barns, and byres, of rough hewn logs, dove-tailed without nails, and the interstices stuffed with moss and turf, to "expel the winter's flaw." The doors and windows in the cabins were placed anyhow, and the latter, at most, had only one or two panes of glass. The roofs were of grass or spruce thatch. Sometimes there was a chimney, but often none, so that smoke issued from many crevices as if they were on fire. The houses were fairly clean within, but, of course, had the reeky flavour so characteristic of everything Russian. The walls were decorated with pictures of the Virgin and unnamed saints; or, per contra, with sheets of the "Illustrated London News," obtained from the Fleet. The essential brick built stove for heating and cooking was always near the door; a few plate racks, boxes, tables, and stools completed the furnishing.

Around the dwellings were a few cleared patches of grass surrounded by wattle fences, but not a single cultivated field or garden. Agriculture was confined to the grazing of a few cows and sheep, and to the rearing of poultry; for all other supplies the people were dependent on Revel. On this account boats with provisions were allowed to come from the latter place every day; and spiritual food in the shape of a priest once a week. Here, as on all the Russian islands visited by the Fleet, the village had a most deserted appearance, only old men, women, and children were visible; all the able-bodied men and boys of the maritime districts having been swept up by the merciless naval conscription, to rot in the pent-up Russian fleet. Ethnologically, the people of these islands were not Russian Slavs, but a mixture of Finns, Swedes, and German Ethonians; they are very fair, blue eyed, and some had the marked Finnish Mongolian expression. Of course, to us they were entirely friendly, as indeed it was their interest to be. But if men were scanty, so were animals; cattle and sheep were few; some lean dogs growled defiance, and a few grey hound pigs trotted about; there were plenty of poultry, shut up in barns from which they kept up an incessant din. On leaving the village we struck through the woods for the lighthouse some six miles away: here and there we came across isolated log cabins; and one excellent but empty chateau, built of sawn timber, with a shingle roof, and superior fittings throughout. The windows were smashed, and inside all was wrack and ruin; it had been an official residence, and, even according to our ideas, a snug and comfortable one. The effects of our ball practice the previous day on the trees skirting the shore were very striking; some were torn and splintered from top to bottom; at the distance of over a mile from the ships we found a 68 pound shot. At a hamlet a party of our Marines were busy washing, using the tubs and boilers of the villagers, who sat by smoking and chatting, quite unconcerned.

We reached the lighthouse about one o'clock, and immediately ascended by 231 steps; a magnificent all round view was our reward; a lookout party from the " Royal George " was in possession, but all the fittings had been carefully removed. We returned to the village about 4 p.m., and had bread and milk and a game at quoits. The Revel priest passed by, and we joked about making him prisoner; he was a pleasant fellow, and he and the

Interpreter had a long conversation in German and Finnish, in the course of which he mentioned that many families, fearing a bombardment, had left Revel. The houses were full of soldiers, and the garrison provisioned for six months. He said the officials blamed the Nargeners for selling us milk, etc., which was obviously absurd; because, we could help ourselves if need be. The people had a keen appreciation of our coin, but if they did not hide it, all would be grabbed by the officials directly our backs were turned.

When we got on board, our own dinner having long been over, Duncan asked me to dine, for the first time, in the Ward Room. I came to the conclusion that, with less pretence, our Gun Room mess was quite as good.

On the 13th, after some days of doubt, we were forced to recognise that loathsome small-pox had broken out on board; whether we brought it from England, or caught it at Faro, was a moot point; but the former was probable, and the strange death at Keil from " malignant measles " was evidently small-pox afterall. The fore part of the upper deck was at once screened off for the isolation of about twenty cases, including Commander Preedy and Lieutenant Poore, R.M.A. Revaccination all round was at once begun.

On this day a curious fog, common in summer in the Gulf of Finland, was seen; in the morning the ship was wholly enveloped; but at noon it lifted for a time about six feet from the water, so that while we could see under it from the Gun Room ports the rest of the ship remained shrouded. It soon re-descended, however, and remained until dispersed in the evening by a westerly breeze.

On the 14th, I attended my first flogging parade, and took particular note of all that passed. In olden times men were flogged, both in the Army and Navy, for trivial offences; but by 1855 it was reserved as a punishment for the more serious crimes.

The culprit in this instance was an ordinary seaman convicted of the despicable offence of stealing from comrades. The whole crew—officers and men—were piped to the quarterdeck, and the culprit paraded to hear the charge, conviction, and sentence read by the Captain. He was ordered to strip, which he did to the waist. A kerchief was bound round his neck, and, standing face on to a trap ribbing, was tied hands and feet to it, like an extended frog. A sturdy boatswain's mate then stepped to the front with a cat o' nine tails, and on signal deliberately delivered twelve lashes, each of which was shouted out and recorded by a ship corporal. He was relieved by another mate; and so on until the forty were administered. The culprit was then unbound, his shirt thrown over his shoulders, and taken to the sick lay for treatment. He bore his punishment pluckily, but evidently suffered much. The effect of the lashes were in order as follows:—the first strokes produced red streaks over the back, and made the muscles visibly quiver; fresh welts continued to arise, till at the end of the first dozen the back was a dull red mass; at the eighteenth the skin broke, and blood began to trickle down, and so on; when the fortieth was reached the back, from the nape of the neck to the loins, was like a lump of bloody meat. I have been at several flogging parades since; but was so deeply impressed by this one, that I wrote in my Journal:

"of all the villainous sights, this is the vilest; yet the terror of the lash prevents an enormous amount of crime on a man o' war." In spite of all the maudlin nonsense which has been written about corporal punishment, it undoubtedly has a deterrent effect on brutalized criminals; witness garrotters.

Meanwhile small-pox had increased to 27 cases including Hannen, the First Lieutenant; and we were ordered to Faro to land the cases, and fumigate the ship. My colleague, More, was placed in charge of them.

On the 17th two deaths occurred on board; seaman McCrea, from anuerism; and Bull, from apoplexy. I moralized over these deaths to the effect that, after all, they were not disproportionate in our ship's population; for it would take a town of 20,000 inhabitants to furnish the able bodied men we had on board. But deaths and small-pox little affected our gaiety; for a sailor whose broken leg I was bandaging said to me in cheery fashion, "Shall I be well for the taking of Cronstadt?" to which I answered "Aye, aye."

On the 18th the "Orion" left at noon, but in the evening, although fifty miles away, we saw her distinctly inverted in the heavens, through mirage.

We left Faro on the 19th and rejoined the Fleet, without the occurrence of any more small-pox.

During the next few days, many, including myself, had shivers and shakes like ague, probably due to great variations in the temperature.

The Queen's birthday was kept with due honour on the 24th; and on the 26th, the Fleet left Nargen, heading up the Gulf of Finland.

CHAPTER IX.

CRONSTADT.

OUR destination now was the renowned Cronstadt, the chief of all the Russian maritime strongholds, in that it blocks the channel to St Petersburg. On Sunday, the 27th, the Fleet was majestically and leisurely steaming in two lines, at a speed of four knots, each big ship towing her respective gunboat. Ahead, the "Amphion" frigate kept a look-out, and on the flanks, paddlewheels carried out a similar duty. In the Gun Room we had just finished a substantial Sunday dinner, and were enjoying siestas on chairs and lockyers, when a cry ran through the ship— "the 'Amphion' signals eleven sail of the enemy in sight." The effect on sleepers and wakers alike was simply electric, and the excitement waxed intense as the Admiral flew the signal— "Proceed at full speed steaming and sailing." The gunboats were cast adrift, and away bowled the liners—each at her best. In a short time eleven sail were plainly visible on the horizon. It was on everybody's lips: have we at last caught our skulking enemies outside their fortifications? Has the long sought chance of an open sea naval engagement at last come? We ran past the island of

Seskar, which was the intended rendezvous, rapidly gaining on the strange sail. The "Duke" kept the lead of the entire Fleet, proving herself not only the biggest but the fastest ship. She was closely followed by the "Orion," "Exmouth," and "Royal George," and yet the maximum speed attained was but 13 knots. What was our disgust, after such high hopes, when the hostile sail resolved themselves into Russian coasting boats, which carry huge spars and canvas for their tonnage! The liners at once gave up chasing such ignoble game, and left the capture to the light paddles.

The Fleet having passed the Seskar anchorage, cast anchor in the open Gulf, in two lines, about 4 p.m.—only sixteen miles from the Tolboukin lighthouse on Cronstadt island. In a short time the lagging gunboats came up, and about 6 p.m. the "Amphion," "Magicienne," and "Merlin" brought in six of the Russian boats, which had been run into a creek at Longi and deserted by their crews.

Several more boats were brought in the following day (including one laden with flour), which were being towed by a tug which cast them adrift and bolted when pursued by the "Magicienne." The boats were all very large, and decked; and were chiefly engaged in the transit of cut wood, which was of much use in the Fleet. When emptied they were moored about 1000 yards away, and used as targets. Those not sunk at practice were set on fire, and being built of highly resinous pine wood made a lively blaze. Only one of the crews belonging to these boats was caught, a big, hairy, real Russian, clad in a long skin coat, whose constant cry was—" I'm a ruined man!"

On the 31st the Fleet proceeded in two lines, slowly and cautiously, towards Cronstadt, and in a few hours there was unfolded before us a magnificent panorama of the great fortress and its surroundings. First, and nearest, was Tolboukin lighthouse, on a reef at the western extremity of Cronstadt island; beyond, the huge granite forts rising out of the water; and behind them the topmasts of the imprisoned Russian Fleet. The town lay at the eastern end of the island, with numerous towers and church spires glittering in the sun. The north and south water channels were bounded by beautifully wooded mainland, that in the south sheltering the royal palace of Orienbaum. The Fleet anchored to the west of Tolboukin, which, deserted by its owners, was entirely at our command.

In the evening the Admiral proceeded to reconnoitre in the small paddlewheel, " Merlin," which had the audacity to go within range of Risbank, but the great fort disdained to fire upon such a tiny if impudent object. In this survey considerably greater depths of water were found than marked on the Russian charts, which were evidently cooked to deter large ships from approaching the forts. In the harbour were counted nine steam vessels, including four line of battle ships ready for action; also a screw frigate, and twelve sailing liners, with topmasts struck and in fighting trim; and, finally, about a dozen sailing liners in various states of unreadiness for sea; but of the whole crowd of ships only one was an actual hulk.

From this it appeared the Russians in Cronstadt

alone had over twenty effective line of battle ships, with which, if they had only had the stomach for fight, they might well have come out and engaged a blockading squadron, at all events inferior in numbers. But discretion was perhaps the better part of valour; for, with what heart could men risk a general action, who displayed such a funk of British sailors, as to allow a gigantic fleet to be imprisoned for weeks by three or four ships of a blockading squadron!

The great fortress of Cronstadt is situated on the long narrow Ketlungi, or Kettle Island, at the mouth of the Neva, and the narrowest neck of the Finland Gulf. On each side of the island are two water channels, but only that on the south is available for large vessels, and this is commanded by cross fire from gigantic forts. The following were the casemated granite faced forts existing in 1855: Risbank 217 guns; Alexander 132; Peter, Constantine, Krouslott or Castle, all rising out of the water; Menchikoff 44 guns, and a number of other batteries on the island. The water batteries were the most formidable, but those on the island itself so completed the defence that the whole place literally bristled with cannon. The garrison numbered 40,000 soldiers and sailors. The north channel, although the wider, was much too shallow to admit of the passage of deep draft ships; but it was also practically entirely blocked by rows of piles at the eastern end. The difficulty and danger of attacking such a place, sheltering a fleet which could deliver a counter stroke, was of course very great; it was therefore clearly our function to imprison the Russian fleet, and paralyse all commerce.

The evening of the day of our arrival before

Fort Risbank 21 Guns as facing the entrance opposite Fort Albo founder as seen from the Fleet June 13 Oct 1833

W.G.D.

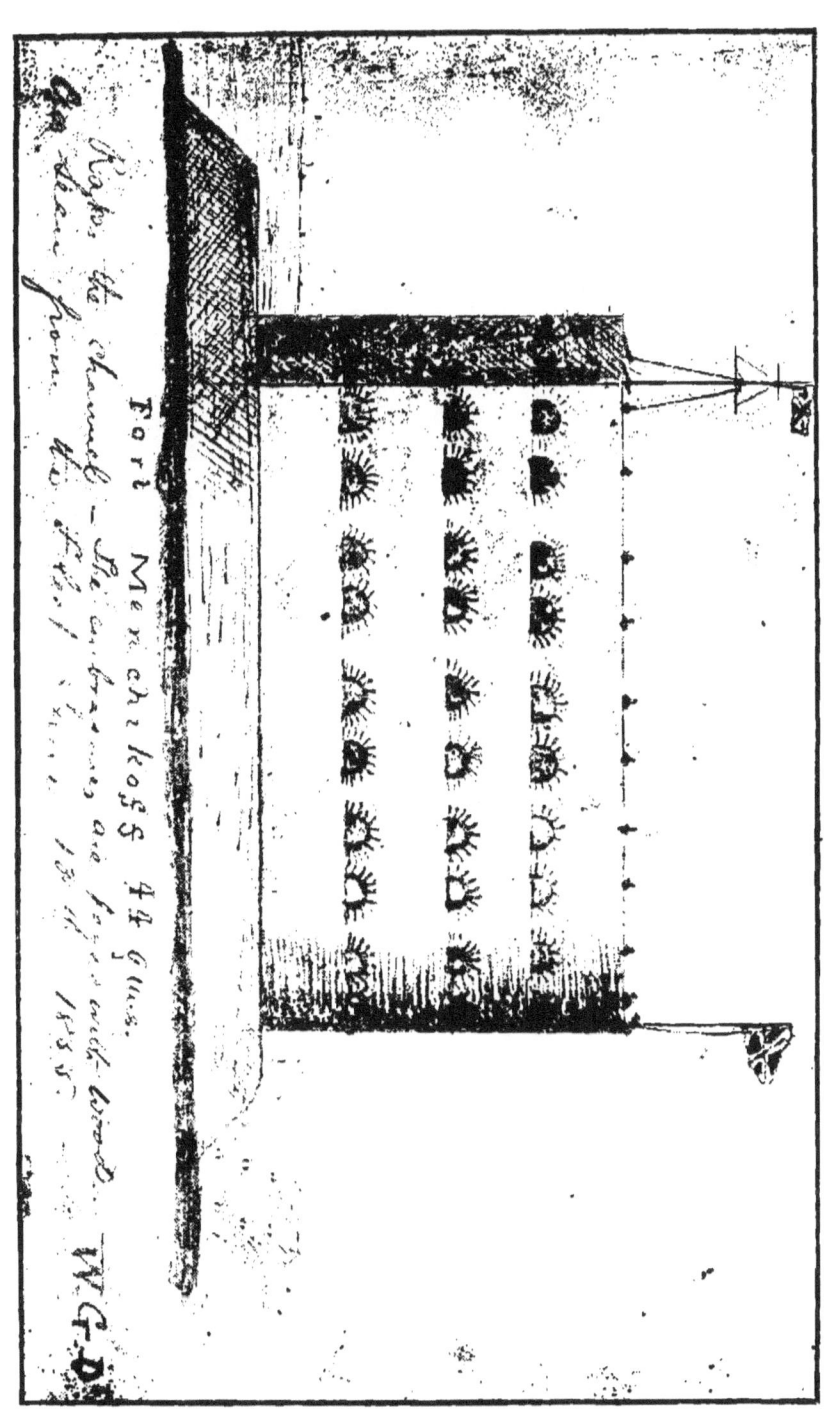

Cronstadt, was superlatively fine, but over the land, in the east, was a mirage, which gave us a wonderful inverted view of St Petersburg itself. The distance to the Imperial City was 25 miles by the winding river, but only 18 as the crow flies; and the whole being a dead level, with a transparent atmosphere, a good view of the street buildings and quays of the capital could be had with a glass from the maintop of a big ship.

With the "glorious first of June" the weather became steady and hotter, and by a suggestive coincidence, we were joined by the French Squadron on that memorable day. It consisted of the screw-liners "Tourville" 86 guns, flagship of Admiral Penaud, "Duquesne" 86 guns, "Austerlitz" 101 guns, and paddlewheel "D'Assas" 28 guns—all of which anchored outside the British line.

Our Admiral being the junior saluted the French flag first, with 21 guns, and the compliment was promptly returned. The Russians were now confronted by the "Allied Fleet."

In the evening the French Admiral visited our Admiral, and was received by the officers in full dress, with a guard of honour; on leaving he received a Rear Admiral's salute of 15 guns, promptly responded to by the "Tourville." And so on the saluting went, till, as I recorded, during the first few days in which the flagships had consorted, 92 guns had been fired and 500 lbs. of gunpowder consumed! Penaud was a nervous, energetic man, just over middle life.

On the 2nd Admiral Dundas reconnoitred the north channel right up to the piles, between which, here and there, a passage for gunboats was left. He went as far as he could in the

"Merlin," and then in a row boat, from which he himself heaved the lead and took soundings with his own hands. Meanwhile dodgy Captain Sullivan of the "Merlin," who was his companion, bouyed the channels between the piles with empty bottles well corked! During these rather hazardous proceedings the boat was almost eastward of Cronstadt, and was able to note the following powerful force in the river way leading to St Petersburg : four two deckers, six frigates, a steam corvettte, bearing an Admiral's flag, and three flotillas, consisting of twenty row gunboats each. Perhaps the Russians were not averse to let the reconnoitring boat have a good look at these formidable obstructions. Thousands of men were also observed employed on earth works on the north side of Cronstadt island, as well as on the opposite mainland.

On the 4th the "Pylades" brought news from Faro that First Lieutenant Hannen had succumbed to small-pox, which gave gallant and popular Hobart his promotion. She also brought three Polish deserters from Revel; artillerymen, clad in long great coats, jack-boots, and flat caps, with a red band and J.P. in front. They said they often looked with longing eyes to the British Fleet last year, but got no opportunity to desert until quite lately; that a large number of the Revel garrison, of 30,000 men, would desert if they could, as they were harshly treated, abominably fed, and in fear of sudden attack were made to sleep under the guns in the cold casemates every night, The poor fellows were loud in their praise of our beef and biscuits, and when given a glass of grog, which they highly prized, drank the Queen's health in Polish, literally as follows : " The health of the

Fort Alexander 132 Guns
Facing the channel opposite Fort Risbank, and supposed to be the strongest of all the Forts. The fort is 50ft high, and would pour a torrent of shot on any ship attempting to force a passage. The above is the appearance as seen from the fleet off Cronstadt June 13th 1855.   W.G.D.

Fort Peter I
Site of Fort Alexander — at its entrance, as this
appeared — as seen from the fleet June 13th 1855

W.G.D.

English Emperor, and may she live long." The men were of average size, fair, and good-looking, but their persons and clothes were filthily dirty, and in spite of the free use of soap and water, long retained the peculiar "gamey" smell of all persons and things Russian.

We had several friendly and unofficial visits from parties of French officers, whose extreme politeness, in bowing, scraping and capering, often provoked our risible faculties. On the 5th the French Admiral and a large party of British and French officers were entertained in the Ward Room of the "Duke"; and after dinner some of the seniors of the Gun Room, including myself, were invited to meet them over wine; the speechifying, singing, chorusing, and general fraternizing were at once comical, hilarious, and almost boisterous.

About this time I recorded, with evident satisfaction, in my Journal, that, although blockading in an enemy's waters, we wanted for nothing in the shape of food. Our supplies of live bullocks, sheep and fowls; together with fresh vegetables, eggs and butter, by the weekly mail from Dautzic, as well as by transports and traders, chiefly from Copenhagen, were very ample. We also regularly received letters, newspapers and telegraphic intelligence, doubtless of a far more authentic and trustworthy kind than that supplied to our Russian opponents over the way.

On the 8th the "Lightning" arrived from Sweaborg with the news of a gross outrage on a flag of truce at Hango Head, by which a boat belonging to the "Cossack" had been captured and the crew killed or made prisoners.

For some time there had been persistent rumours

that the Russians had laid down what were scornfully called "infernal machines," in the waterways about Cronstadt; but it was hardly credited they could resort to such infamous and unnaval weapons. Truly, the torpedoes and submarine mining of these latter days were then little anticipated!

But on the 9th rumour became reality, for two sudden submarine explosions occurred under the "Merlin" while cruising in the north channel, and a third, almost at the same moment, under the bows of a gunboat with her. Neither vessel sustained any material injury, but the existence of submerged diabolical machines was no longer in doubt. No attempt was then made to dredge up and examine these detestable inventions.

As midsummer was now approaching, the days became excessively hot on board, but the nights remained fairly cool.

Our active cruiser, the "Magicienne," on the 12th, approached the south mainland shore, west of Cronstadt, and immediately some peripatetic field artillery were brought to bear on her. The duel was interesting, but the ship very soon proved to have the best of it.

Accidents were very frequent on board, occasionally of a fatal character, and of this kind I witnessed a very sad one on the 13th. A man, painting the outside of the ship at the upper deck, suddenly fell feet foremost, past the Gun Room port where I chanced to be seated, into the water. When we looked out only his cap and paint brushes were to be seen floating. He never came up, nor was the body recovered. The poor fellow was supposed to have at once sunk deep in the muddy bottom which held him fast.

CHAPTER X.

INFERNAL MACHINES.

ON the 14th June, the Allied Fleet, with the exception of three English blockships of 60 guns, proceeded down the gulf to Seskar island, off which it anchored the same afternoon. The exact object of this move I never learned, but it was probably for the sake of a little change, and a pleasant one it was. On the 16th a large number of British and French officers landed for a ramble, and made straight for the chief village in the centre of the island. It was intensely hot in the thick woods, but presently we came across a delightful cool meadow, brilliant with flowers, and buzzing with bees and other insects. The village close by was much larger, and the houses greatly superior to any on Nargen, but looked equally forlorn and deserted: we were told that no less than 300 men and boys, from 8 to 50 years of age, had been drafted away under the conscription; and consequently only old men, women, and children were left. Some of the girls were pretty, but the young women decidedly plain, and the old veritable hags.

I gave a little, flaxen-haired maiden some bits of ship biscuit, for which she innocently kissed my hand. They repudiated being Russians, and called themselves, with much emphasis, "Finsk"—that is Fins.

The furniture of the houses usually comprised a few stools, some small tables fitted with deep drawers, two or more large boxes, which also served as bedsteads, and a plate rack. Near the door was the usual plastered stove, containing a bread oven, and having a few cooking utensils atop. Spruce beer, which they offered us, was the gala drink, but it had a turpentine smell and flavour. A large number of sledge dogs and domestic cats were about, as well as a few cows and pigs; and the poultry, probably for fear of Fleet foragers, were shut up as at Nargen, but they were much in evidence through crowing and cackling.

The chief building was the church, built of dressed wood, and having a small tower or steeple. It was full of pictures, representing Christ, the Crucifixion, the Baptist, Virgin, and Russian Saints. The altar was enveloped in gold-embroidered, shabby, black velvet, and on a wall adjoining hung the incongruous barbaric outfit of the priests, consisting of sundry seedy vestments, two enormous cocked hats, a wreath of ribbons, and a couple of swords. The uses of these paraphernalia puzzled us. Bibles and prayer books, in Russian, were scattered about; and at the door hung a poor box containing a few brass copecks, to which we added some silver of a better coinage. We behaved with becoming decency in the church, and the only constructive sacrilege was climbing the steeple and ringing the fine toned bell!

On the 18th the Russian version of the Hango Head affair arrived, differing materially from ours.

They declared there was no flag of truce; that the fight was fair; six of the boat's crew were killed, and the rest, nearly all wounded, taken prisoners. We thought the Russians protested a little too much, however.

On this glorious midsummer night we skylarked by permission on the quarter deck until 11.30, and it was quite bright—only a fading light as in an eclipse.

On the 19th the liners, "Exmouth" and "Blenheim," with the gunboats, "Gleaner" and "Pincher," bombarded and destroyed some earthworks at Narva, a town on the south shore, nearly opposite to Seskar.

On the 20th, the combined fleet, in two lines, led by the "Duke" and "Exmouth," returned to Cronstadt. On approaching Tolboukin, about 3 p.m., we passed our former anchorage, and boldly steamed up the north channel, regardless alike of supposed shoals and infernal machines, until due north of Cronstadt town; 2½ miles from the shore, and 3½ from St Andrew's Church.

This unexpected move greatly disconcerted the Russians, who had not discounted the possibility of great ships, at least, venturing into such shallow waters; and so they might, for we were close to the muddy bottom. Great commotion was visible in and about the fortress; bright helmets were at every corner; white coated soldiers crowded the ramparts; troops in masses hurried to and fro; orderlies galloped about; civilian sight-seers occupied every point of vantage; and no less than 14 steamers and 16 gunboats were counted puffing about. Beyond the piles, on the Neva proper, several tourist steamers from St Petersburg were crowded from stem to stern.

We had indeed woke up the whole place, and it was evident an immediate attack was expected on the north, which was the weakest side of Cronstadt.

About 8 p.m., while the "Vulture," 6 guns, was taking up position ahead of the "Duke," an infernal machine exploded under her bows; it did no harm, but reminded us we were indeed in the very hornet's nest.

Next day boats were sent out, the first thing, to fish us these submarine pests, of which no less than eight were hooked by the "Duke." All this was most sensational, and in the evening I recorded in my Journal: "This has been a most eventful day, in the capture of infernal machines, and from both our Admirals meeting with accidents while examining them."

These were the circumstances alluded to.

The first machine brought on board the "Duke" was deprived of its fuse, swung at a boom end, and fired at with a rifle, to see whether it would explode by mere concussion, but without result. It was then brought down to the poop for dissection, and was found to consist of an automatic exploding mechanism at one end, and a charge of about 8 lbs. of coarse gunpowder at the other.

Meanwhile, Admiral Seymour on board the "Exmouth" was manipulating an intact machine, which exploded, injuring his eyes and face, as well as the persons of some of the onlookers. This explosion startled us, and before we had time to reflect, a loud report came from our own Admiral's cabin, but being only the bursting of a fuse did no harm. A self-constituted Committee, of which I formed one, was immediately assembled to scientifically examine and report on these dangerous bombs; with the following results: The case was a cone of zinc 20 inches long, by 14 at base, the latter forming an air chamber, while the apex ended in a ring by which it was anchored downward; this arrangement enabled it to float base upwards a foot or two under water. The fuse was inserted in a solid zinc tube in the centre of the base, and protruding from it; which tube passed through the air chamber to that containing the gunpowder at the apex, and was rigid and fixed throughout; the enclosed fuse consisted of a moveable copper tube, which embraced at its lower end a very thin lead tube, which surrounded one of fragile glass containing sulphuric acid, and this rested on a pad of cotton wool saturated with chlorate of potash. These chemical reagents were brought into contact as follows: round the exterior base of the machine a number of wire rods projected, which converged on, and entered the zinc tube through holes: if any of these rods were driven inwards they struck the moveable copper tube, tilting it, thereby bending the lead and breaking the glass tubes; this released the acid on the chlorate, instantly producing flame, and exploding the gunpowder. The whole was the invention of a St Petersburg Professor (Jacobi), and was more mechanically ingenious than chemically recondite. Indeed, some of the Anarchist bombs have recently (1894) been exploded by identically similar means. The machines were probably intended quite as much to frighten as to hurt; but in these days of torpedoes and submarine mining with high explosives, are now sufficiently ridiculous. I constructed a pasteboard model of one which I brought home.

On the 24th a very strong, warm, east wind

showed us the danger of our position by blowing the water down the Gulf, and lessening the depth around our anchorage by nearly a fathom and a half.

During the next week speculation was busy and rumour rife as to the intentions of the Admirals; but, as the complement of the gun and mortar boats, though daily arriving from England, was not complete, it became evident nothing much would be done until they had all mustered.

Our chief excitement was in the capture of Russian coasting craft, which were constantly trying to evade our cruisers, and sneak up to St Petersburg close inshore. Some of those taken were laden with Government cartridge paper and pasteboard from the Finnish factories.

On the 29th we enlivened the Russians by general quarters, with shell practice, which they watched with feverish and critical eyes.

On the 30th I landed at Tolboukin with Naylor, R.M., and Banks, and a party of ex-small-pox patients from Faro for clothes washing. The lighthouse was beautifully built, and, of course, dismantled, but both it and its outhouses in perfect order. I made a sketch of the place. On ascending to the top we had a magnificent view of everything connected with Cronstadt and its surroundings; and the marvel was that the Russians should have left standing such a point of vantage at our command. Scattered around the building were enormous four feet cubes of red granite, which had been brought hither on the ice in winter for the building of the casemated forts. We dined at noon on board our escort, the " Starling," gunboat to the " Duke," commanded by Prince Leningen, nephew to Queen Victoria. He was a hospitable

TOLBOUKIN LIGHTHOUSE. SKETCHED JUNE 30TH, 1855.

fellow. On returning to Tolboukin in the evening we found our party increased by two Russian deserters from the "St Michael," three decker, lying between the forts. Seeing us at the lighthouse, they somehow managed to escape in a fishing boat.

On the 1st July the Russians made a return performance of shell practice, in our direction, from some earthworks on the north of the island, but none of their missiles came near us. Next day we watched a lively duel between the gunboats "Thistle" and "Gleaner," and field artillery on the southern shore; during which some wood caught fire and burned furiously for hours. In the evening a Russian Sergeant, a German, managed to desert to the Fleet, and gave us much information. He said there were 30,000 sailors and soldiers in Cronstadt, and great numbers of visitors came daily from St Petersburg to view the Fleet, at a return fare of two roubles.

We had lately been joined by several pleasure yachts from England, and also by traders from various ports. One enterprising Dundee skipper flew from his little barque a huge flag labelled "Provisions." The weather was now uncomfortably hot, and white duck trousers were taken into wear. On the evening of the 4th a number of armed boats from the liners went to the north shore to practice blank firing, and succeeded in greatly alarming the Russians.

On the 6th Captain Boyd of the "Royal George" fitted one of the stoutest recently captured galliots with a 32 pounder, pointing through the hatchway at an angle of 40 degrees, with which he first fired a few shots which reached the shore at an extreme range of three miles. The "Thistle" then towed the craft to within 2,500 yards of an earthwork to the west of Cronstadt town, into which a few shells were thrown, and even one or two into a wood far in its rear ; the enemy, tickled and angered, replied savagely, but only one shot came within fifty yards of the galliot.

On the evening of the 10th, while we were having a dance on the quarterdeck with some French officers, the "Magicienne" brought a boat, captured at Systerback, alongside, containing three men and two women, Fins ; the former came on board with confidence, but the poor women crouched in terror in the boat : but soon regained confidence when hoisted on board, and given a glass of sherry. Instead of being hanged, they were liberally supplied with provisions, and towed home rejoicing. What could they have thought of the gay scene they witnessed on the Flagship?

The 13th was the Russian Empress's birthday. Cronstadt was gaily decked with bunting, and salutes fired. Balloons were sent up from St Petersburg : in the evening huge bonfires blazed along the shore, and salvoes of guns and rockets were discharged till midnight. Watching this display, I was struck with the drawing in of daylight, as it was nearly dark by 11 o'clock.

On the 14th the entire Fleet weighed, and soon was in motion. The enemy thought the long expected attack was to begin, and great was the commotion everywhere. But the ships merely steamed quietly to the old anchorage west of the Tolboukin, and all dropped their anchors except the "Duke," "Exmouth," "Tourville," and

"Austerlitz," which slipped away down the Gulf.

Thus came to an end, as far as we were concerned, a continuous blockade of three weeks of Cronstadt, which we were evidently not going to attack, and which I saw no more.

CHAPTER XI.

PREPARATIONS AGAINST SWEABORG.

ALTHOUGH the bulk of the Fleet was left behind, yet, as we bore away the three Admirals, British and French, we rightly inferred the intended stroke was to be delivered elsewhere than at Cronstadt. At 1 p.m. we passed the friendly island of Seskar: at 5 sighted Levonsari: and at 8 skirted Hochland (Highland) on which the most prominent object was the Governor's mansion embosomed in woods.

Early next morning the "Duke" and "Tourville" anchored in the old spot at Nargen, having made the run of 210 miles in 21 hours, but the slower "Exmouth" and "Austerlitz" only turned up during the forenoon. Here we found the blockships, "Russell," "Cornwallis," and " Pembroke," some paddles, and several gunboats, both French and English: also fifteen mortar boats, and a large convoy of traders and colliers.

On the 16th the "Arrogant" reported having had a sharp engagement with riflemen in a wood at Biorka, during which a rocket exploded the wrong way, smashing a boat, injuring several men, and causing the death by drowning of a midshipman named Story.

We found Nargen much cooler than Cronstadt. As it was by the mortars we hoped to astonish the Russians, we were deeply interested in successful trial of them, which was made on the 17th. Each shell had a diameter of 13 inches, and a bursting charge of 20 lbs. of powder. They were propelled by a like charge, at an angle of 45 degrees, and at a range of about 4000 yards attained an elevation of about 1000 feet. From this altitude they thundered sheer down, bursting either near the ground and scattering destructive fragments over an area of 500 square yards, or first embedding themselves, and then exploding with the force of a small mine. These shells were by far the most formidable engines of destruction then known.

The same evening we entertained a large party of French officers in the Gun Room, and our resourceful steward, Mr Whitcomb, surpassed himself in the sumptuousness of the menu. There was much fraternizing and such toasts as the

Queen, and the Emperor, and the "Alliance," drunk with wild enthusiasm.

On the 19th the Admirals went off in the "Merlin" to have a look at Sweaborg, which we concluded was to be the real object of our attentions; they returned in the evening, with the information that the Russians, as at Sebastopool, were making desperate efforts to block the navigable channel by sinking their war ships. Next day Revel was surveyed, and pronounced by Colonel Travers less assailable than Sweaborg, because it could not be attacked in detail.

Meanwhile the gun and mortar boats were painted lead colour to make them less visible at a distance.

The 20th, on shore at Nargen, was an intensely hot day, but the pretty flowers, bonny blue bells, and luscious blae berries in the woods made me feel quite at home.

We watched several trim and pleasant faced Swedish lasses making hay. Many Frenchmen were strolling about, but it was quite evident we were far more popular with the natives than they. I espied a French midshipman in a house discussing a bowl of milk, and called for one myself; there was sixpence each to pay; my requisite silver coin was received with polite bows; but the national copper which the Frenchman tendered was rejected with "no goot," "no goet;" nevertheless he quietly tabled it and walked away.

Of not a few accidents I witnessed on the "Duke," the saddest, perhaps, was on the 23rd; a seaman named Murdoch Mackenzie, from the Isle of Skye, fell during drill from the mainyard to the quarterdeck, which although only 50 or 60 feet, entailed an awful smash: the thigh and wrist bones protruded, and scarcely a large bone was left whole in his body: he only breathed a few minutes: Alas! for his poor Highland mother of whom he was said to be the stay!

We heard this day of a sharp fight between some of our smaller vessels, and the enemy's earthworks at Frederickshaven.

About this time the "Calcutta" sailing 84, arrived from England with a number of armed boats, and the "Æolus" with shot and shell, all of which looked like business.

I went on shore every day, and much enjoyed strolling in the woods and picking the dainty blaeberries. At the Sexton's house, adjoining the cemetery, a restaurant was started, where coffee, milk, beer, bread and cheese, could be had on reasonable terms. I, of course, explored the cemetery, which contained the graves of quite a large number of men of our 1854 Baltic Fleet; each was marked with a plain wooden cross. But this remote place also held the bones of some of our countrymen interred half a century before: on a decayed piece of wood I found, faintly visible, the following inscription: "In memory of William Sinclair belonging to His Britannic Majesty's Ship St George." This indeed, was a relic of one of Nelson's line of battle ships, which he passed into the Baltic in 1801, in search of the Swedish Fleet, during the political complications following the bombardment of Copenhagen.

If our blockade of Revel was effective in regard to warlike and trading vessels, it was less rigorous for individuals; for one day I saw a party of young fellows in Nargen, over from Revel on a visit to their friends, cooly drinking, smoking, and playing cards.

At last, on the 31st, we were immensely delighted with the definite announcement of a contemplated grand attack on Sweaborg. In preparation for this, during the first days of August, all the vessels were busy filling up with shot and shell. The quantity of warlike stores to draw on was prodigious, as witness the following entry in my Journal :—" I am informed there is actually more gunpowder in the Fleet than was sent to or expended by the Duke of Wellington's army during the whole Peninsular War!"

I recorded a complete list, copied from official documents, of the Allied Fleet in the Baltic at this time, as follows :—

BRITISH.

LINERS.	GUNS.	CAPTAINS.
Duke of Wellington,*	131	H. Caldwell.
Royal George,	101	H. Codrington.
Exmouth,*	91	W. K. Hall.
Nile,	91	G. R. Mundy.
Orion,	91	J. E. Erskine.
James Watt,	91	G. Elliot.
Cæsar,	91	J. Robb.
Majestic,	81	J. Hope.
Cressy,	81	R. L. Warren.
Colossus,	81	R. L. Robinson.
Pembroke,†	60	G. H. Seymour.
Cornwallis,†	60	G. D. Wellesley.
Ajax,†	60	F. Warden.
Hawke,†	60	E. Ommaney.
Russell,†	60	F. Scott.
Blenheim,†	60	W. H. Hall.
Edinburgh,†	60	R. S. Hewlett.
Hastings,†	60	J. C. Caffin.
Hogue,†	60	W. Ramsay.
Sanspariel,‡	71	...
No. 19.	1470	

* Flagships.   † Blockships.   ‡ Not arrived.

BALTIC FLEET OF 1855.

GUNBOATS.	COMMANDERS.	MORTAR BOATS.
Starling,	Prince Leningen.	Rocket.
Thistle,	... D. Spain. ...	Pickle.
Lark,	... M. Pechell....	Surly.
Redwing,	C. S. Forbes.	Blazer.
Magpie,	... B. Pim. ...	Mastiff.
Snap,	...C. A. Wise....	Porpoise.
Weasel,	...R. Craigie. ...	Sinbad.
Ruby,	...H. G. Hale....	Manly.
Pelter,	... W. F. Lee. ...	Drake.
Dapper,	H. J. Grant.	Prompt.
Stork,	G. H. Malcolm.	Carron.
Hind,	Lord E. Cecil.	... Redbreast.
Gleaner,	...A S. Bogle....	
Biter,	W. H. Anderson.	Beacon.
Skylark,	.. F. W. Pym....	Havock.
Pincher,	...R. Stewart....	
Snapper,	... A. Villiers. ...	Growler.
Swinger,	Hon. M. H. Nelson.	Grappler.
Badger	W. Cumming.	
No. 20.		No. 16.

FRIGATES.	GUNS.	CAPTAINS.
Imperieuse,	51	R. B. Watson.
Euryalus,	51	... G. Ramsay.
Arrogant,	47	H. R. Yelverton.
Amphion,	34	... A. C. Key.
Retribution,	28	... T. Fisher.
No. 5.	211	

CORVETTES.	GUNS.	
Cossack,	21	E. F. Fanshaw.
Tartar,	21	... H. Dunlop.
Pylades,	21	E. D'Eyncourt.
Esk,	21	T. F. Birch.
Harrier,	17	... H. Story.
Falcon,	17	W. J. S. Pullen.
Cruiser,	17	Hon. G. Douglas.
Conflict,	8	F. C. Brown.
Archer,	8	E. Heathcote.
Desperate,	8	R. D. White.
No. 10.	159	

PADDLES.	GUNS.	CAPTAINS.
Magicienne,	16	N. Vausittart.
Vulture,	6	F. H. N. Glass.
Dragon,	6	W. Stewart.
Geyser,	6	Rhoderick Dew.
Bulldog,	6	A C. Gordon.
Driver,	6	A. H. Gardner.
Basilisk,	6	R. Jenner.
Centaur,	6	W. C. Clifford.
Merlin,	4	R. Sullivan.
Cuckoo,	3	A. C. Murray.
Locust,	3	A. Bythesea.
Porcupine,	3	R. M. Jackson.
No. 12.	77	

Bellisle (Hospital), ... J. Hoskins.
Eolus (shot and shell), ... W. S. Brown, Master.
Volage (powder), ... H. Hitchins, Master.
Volcano (factory), ... J. Ryan, Master.
Lightning (Tender), J. C. Campbell, Commander.
Princess Alice (Tender), J. Underwood, Commander.

Ships, 52 ⎫
Gunboats, 19 ⎬ 87
Mortar boats, 16 ⎭

Guns, 1997. Mortars, 16. Crews, 24,000.

FRENCH.

LINERS.	GUNS.	
Tourville,	86	Flagship of Admiral Penaud.
Duquesne,	86	
Austerlitz,	101	
(3)		
PADDLES.		Ships, 6 ⎫
D'Assas,	28	Gunboats, 4 ⎬ 15
Pelican,	4	Mortars, 5 ⎭
(2)		Guns, 221.
GUNBOATS.		Mortars. 5.
L'Aigle,	4	Crews, 2500.
L'Avalanche,	4	
Le Dragon,	4	
Le Tempete,	4	
(4)		

Mortars, 5. Hospital Ship, 1.

Total of Allied Fleets.—Ships, 102; Guns, 2218; Mortars, 20; Crews, 26,500.

The British gunboats were armed with two long solid 68 pounders, and two 24 pound howitzers; the Mortar boats with one 13 inch mortar each; and both had crews of 30 men; but as the boats were all attached to line of battle ships, the crews were interchangeable among the ships. The Gunboat squadron were commanded by Lieutenants, and collectively by Commander Preedy of the " Duke ;" the Mortar boats by Mates, and for mortar firing were grouped in two divisions under Captains Lawrence and Schomberg, and collectively under Captain Wemyss—all of the Royal Marine Artillery. The French mortars were 10 inch, but they had several spare ones which they used on an island at Sweaborg.

The force in the Baltic was therefore very strong; but it was, of course, much scattered, cruising here, blockading there.

The evening of the 3rd August, preceding our sailing on the morrow, was very festive on the ships going to Sweaborg; all longed for a chance at the Russians, which had never been had fair during the two years of the war.

But our hopes were dashed, for daylight of the 4th broke with a violent westerly gale, which prevented the very mixed Fleet moving off until the morning of the 6th, which it then did in splendid weather, destined to last until we had finished with Sweaborg. On that day, at 3 p.m., we sighted the fortified islands, collectively called Sweaborg, which has been well named the Gibraltar of the North. Approaching with caution, we anchored, at 4 p.m., almost due west of the fortress, and south of Helsingfors on the mainland, at a general distance of about 5000 yards from the batteries. The proper entrance to

Sweaborg harbour is from the south; but we were in shallow waters, studded with islands, islets, and bare projecting rocks, in what would have proved an uncommon tight place in bad weather. Into this position the Fleet was led by the gigantic "Duke," much, as at Cronstadt, to the astonishment of the Russians, who never expected big ships would venture into such an anchorage. Yet, there we were, and, as it was evident we meant mischief, great was the commotion in the fortress.

The night of arrival was very dark, and watch boats were sent out on every side. The morning of the 7th broke clear and beautiful, and unfolded a magnificent panorama of town, fortress, and adjacent coasts. I remarked, a description of compact Cronstadt was easy, but it was very different with scattered Sweaborg.

Due north lay Helsingfors, the gay capital of Finland, a university city of 25,000 inhabitants; having many fine public and private buildings. The Cathedral was very prominent, having a great central dome, and at the angles smaller ones with minarets; all gaudily painted and gilded after the semi-oriental fashion of Russian churches. On heights near the town an army of about 10,000 men were paraded, to show us what we might expect on a landing. On slopes between the town and shore were great civilian crowds intently scanning and watching the Fleet; with many ladies, in gay summer attire, carrying brilliantly coloured parasols to shield from the glaring sun.

West of the town we espied, over a large red building, a gigantic hoarding, on which was painted in English, in huge letters, "Lunatic Asylum."

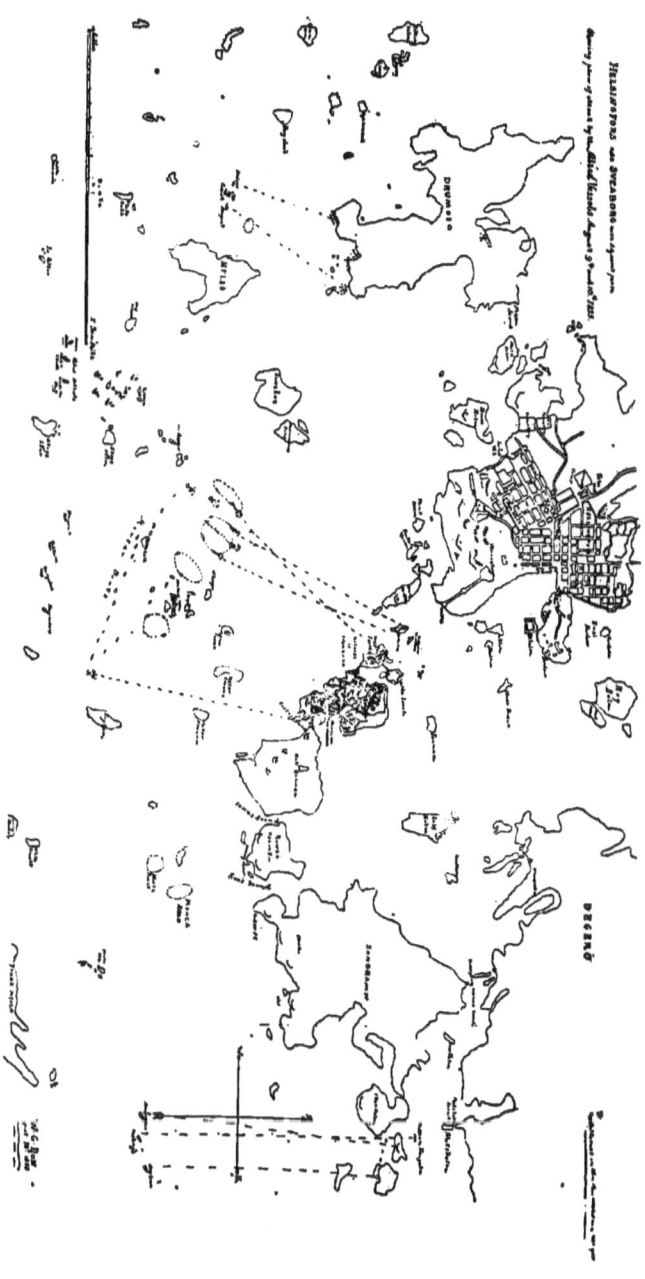

We were really hard-hearted and incredulous enough to suspect said building more probably contained war-like stores than madmen!

Eastward, on the road to Sweaborg, another large white building was recognized as the Government Observatory. From the position we occupied, and despite Sweaborg, we could easily have destroyed Helsingfors and all it contained.

The fortifications of Sweaborg, in 1855, extended over seven different islands; with earthworks also on several others, notably Holman and Sandhamn.

Vargon was the central and citadel island, and south of it Gustafsvard commanded the narrow entrance to the naval harbour, which was enclosed by the various islands. North of Vargon was East, West, and Little Svarto, and also Langhorn and Rantan, all of which were very heavily armed. Vargon and Gustafsvard, being precipitous, had casemates cut in the solid rock, while the other forts were built of massive granite. The whole mounted 800 guns, with converging and cross fire in every direction open to attack. On the various fortified islands were immense barracks for a garrison of 12,000 men; also dockyard stores, magazines, hospitals, and prisons. Very large gas works were situate on West Svarto. The narrow entrance to the harbour was blocked by sunken ships. The whole coast is so cut up and surrounded by wooded islands and peninsulas, making approach doubly difficult, that Sir Charles Napier, in 1854, pronounced Sweaborg impregnable, both by sea and land.

I was permitted to trace a chart in the Admiral's

office, which showed the position of the chief magazines. The largest was on Gustafsvard, in a ravine, surmounted by casemated batteries, and earth bastions a-top; four were on Vargon, and two in East Svarto. It is needless to say all of these were about to engage the polite and sedulous attention of our mortar fire.

The vessels which took part in the bombardment of Sweaborg were the following:—

BRITISH.

LINERS.—Duke of Wellington, Exmouth, Hastings, Edinburgh, Pembroke, Cornwallis, Bellisle.

FRIGATES.—Euryalus, Arrogant, Amphion, Æolus.

CORVETTES and PADDLES.—Cossack, Cruiser, Magicienne, Vulture, Geyser, Dragon, Merlin, Lightning, Princess Alice, Volcano.

GUNBOATS.—All, except Ruby, Hind, and Swinger.

MORTAR BOATS.—All.

FRENCH.

LINERS.—Austerlitz, Tourville, Duquesne.

FRIGATE and STEAMERS.—Hospital Frigate, Pelican.

GUNBOATS.—All.

MORTAR BOATS.—All.

Giving a total of 69 vessels.

On the evening of the 7th our reconnoitring boats drew some shells from Vargon, which were the first hostile shots. Meanwhile, the French were busy erecting a mortar battery, on an islet called Otterhall or Abramsholm, within easy range of Gustafsvard, which was finished without molestation, because undetected. On the forenoon of the 8th the Russian Royal Standard was unfurled on Vargon, indicating Imperial presence; which was none other than the Grand Duke Constantine, head of the Navy, a man notorious for his Muscovite arrogance and bumptiousness, which it was our especial desire to take down. The final dispositions of attack were made this day; the battle ships and larger vessels were anchored in an outer circle south and west of Sweaborg, at about 4600 yards; the mortar boats inside, at about 3300 yards, but having 400 fathoms of cable to haul and veer on, out and in, according as the enemy might too accurately get their range, a most admirable, and, as it proved, effective safeguard; the gunboats inside of all fighting in constantly moving circles, a plan by which the range of the Russians was completely baffled. The French rock battery bore heavily on Gustafsvard at 2,300 yards.

On the left the corvettes "Cossack" and "Cruiser" commanded some closely adjacent wooded islands; and on the extreme right, opposite the entrance to the harbour, the "Hastings," the "Cornwallis," and the "Amphion" guarded against attack from that direction. Outside the fighting line were anchored a few traders and colliers, and some pleasure yachts, among which I have preserved the names "Pandora" and "Wee Pet."

Although the naval force threatening Sweaborg was both formidable and unique in the possession of powerful mortars, yet the issue of an attack was very problematical; and the experience of ships versus forts at Sebastopol not assuring. Was the Baltic Fleet to be ingloriously repulsed, and add defeat to the already unjust charge of inactivity?

But uncertainties like these did not weigh heavily on us; for after supper we shouted confidence and defiance in " Rule Britannia " and " God save the Queen," and then turned in, to be piped up at a very early hour.

CHAPTER XII.

BOMBARDMENT OF SWEABORG.

AT dawn on the 9th August the ship was aroused at 3.30. Very soon after, we saw the sun rise in glory right over the stately and unbroken fortress, which was so speedily to become a ruin and desolation. The morning light brightly gilded a peaceful scene, which before noon was to be darkened with the horrors of war!

At 5 a.m. the "Duke" hauled in a few hundred yards nearer the line of mortar boats, so as to command better signalling distance ; and at the same time the Admiral and Commodore made a cruise in the "Merlin" to inspect the fighting line.

By 7 all was ready for the opening of the bombardment, and at 7.30 Captain Wemyss gave the signal by firing a shell from the "Pickle." As every mortar was loaded, the response was immediate and terrific. With a simultaneous roar about five and twenty huge shells sped away, and mounting up, until over Vargon and Gustafsvard, thundered straight down upon them with destructive effect.

Of the opening salvo, one or two exploded short or went over among the shipping in the harbour, but the majority crashed down where intended, right over the magazines, and, on bursting, threw up columns of white smoke, mingled with dark earth and rubbish. At the same moment as the mortars, the gunboats also opened a very heavy fire on the forts of shot and shell from their 68 pounders. The Russian reply was immediate and appalling; as if by magic the smoke of heavy guns issued from every nook and point, high and low, all over the islands, from hundreds of cannon and mortars; a perfect storm of shot, hot and cold, and shell at all angles of cross fire, came towards us, hissing, splashing, ricochetting in every direction. If that awful shower of missles had reached us with effect, we should, indeed, have been in a bad way! Fortunately, it did us no practical harm, but some of the gunboats had narrow escapes; and even a few shells burst uncomfortably near the "Duke," splashing up the water around. With such salvos the furious duel continued unflagging for quite an hour; at the end of which, while only a few of our gunboats had been lightly hit, we could visibly see that our fire was telling with cumulative effect; so that by 8.30 the fire from some of the Russian forts and earthworks, which were becoming untenable, considerably slackened. The allied gunners had so perfected their range that hardly a shot or shell was wasted; while the Russian practice became wilder, just as it was found impossible to hit the constantly moving gun and mortar boats.

At 9 a.m. the "Cornwallis," "Hastings," and "Amphion" on the far right bore in on some earthworks at Sandhamn, and opened heavy broadside fire. They approached the batteries within 700 yards; but, as these were situated on a high bank, the ships could not sufficiently elevate their guns to sweep them, and were therefore so peppered as to be forced to haul out twice, finally retiring after an hour, with a number of wounded, but no killed. The " Cornwallis " was hulled nineteen times. The object of this attack was to distract and harass the enemy.

Shortly after 9 it was becoming very evident our shell fire was having terrible effect, especially on Vargon, from which, as the barracks, stores, and various buildings caught fire in detail, dense columns of smoke began to arise. The magazines also were becoming denuded of the earth masses atop through the explosion of our embedded shells. Altogether our fire was constant and relentless ; while that of the Russians was fitful and almost ineffective. At 10.30 our shells reached a magazine, and a prodigious cloud of white smoke arose over Vargon; from which emerged dark masses of stones, guns, and even men's bodies. It was followed by a noise like thunder, and a heavy concussion as of an earthquake. When the smoke cleared away, one of the great forts was disclosed a ruin, at which our men manned the rigging and cheered. The tremendous nature of the explosion so frightened the sight-seers, especially the ladies, at Helsingfors that they scuttled off in every direction.

Meanwhile, about 11 a.m., a number of riflemen opened fire on the ships from the wooded island of Drumsio, which was near our left, and sent a shower of bullets over and around us. Such impudence was beyond a joke, and the corvettes " Cossack " and " Cruiser," immediately opened on the wood, through which every shot from their 8 inch guns cut a lane. Needless to say the riflemen soon made themselves scarce.

For a short time after the Vargon explosion the Russians were much disconcerted, and fired very irregularly; but our fire never slackened at all, except when the crews of the gun and mortar boats were being relieved by fresh men from the liners. Many of the artillerymen on return from the mortar boats were quite deaf from the continued heavy discharges.

On the stroke of noon a second but much smaller explosion occurred, also on Vargon. We had gone below to dinner, but had hardly sat down, when great shouts and commotion overhead caused a simultaneous rush on deck, to witness a spectacle on Vargon and Gustafsvard which altogether baffled description, and before which all stood for a time appalled. Grant, in " British Battles," compared the scene to " the eruption of a volcano," and called it a " veritable pandemonium," which in truth it was. Magazine after magazine, in succession, was exploding with a violence which shook both sea and land for a great distance around. Huge masses of stones, guns, shot and shell, and human bodies were hurled in the air, to descend in a mingled shower. As Grant says—" Had the isle been torn from its granite base in the sea the roar of that explosion could not have been more terrific and astounding"; so appalling was it that everyone's attention was for a time rivetted, and the firing on both sides ceased for a few minutes; but this lull was succeeded by such tremendous cheering as must have been almost audible on shore, and a renewal of our fire with increased and incomparable vigour; while the Russians, as well they might, seemed paralysed.

When the smoke cleared away, the site of the great magazine between Vargon and Gustafsvard was revealed like a great quarry hole, with every vestige of the forts and earthworks atop gone. It was evident, that, given time and sufficient means, Sweaborg, and even Cronstadt, could be destroyed with comparative impunity to ourselves.

The Russians soon regained confidence, and began to fire very savagely in response to our hammer and tongs; and so, throughout the afternoon, while our fire was steady and most destructive, their's was at times intermittent, and always ineffective. Only four of our gunboats had yet been hit, and not one put out of action. About two o'clock the conflagration extended to the Svartos, and by 3.30 the Admiralty, and at 4 the Citadel were burning furiously; later on, extensive areas in the islands were covered with the flames of burning buildings. Just before dark, the Russians kept up an incessant cannonade with much desperation, and then ceased altogether; our gunboats also ceased; but not the mortars, which throughout the night threw one shell every five minutes.

At 9 p.m. a large number of armed boats from the liners rowed to within 1500 yards of the fortress, and poured in a heavy shower of rockets for about two hours. As soon as a rocket arose the Russians fired on the apparent spot, and some of the boats had very narrow escapes from destruction. The rocket practice was a splendid sight, and these missiles, with heavy bursting charges, soon started fresh conflagrations in places that had hitherto escaped. The boats returned to the ships at midnight, with very few casualties, but all mightily tired, and ready to turn in. Before going below I took one more look at the burning fortress, but words could not paint the scene. Like the cities of the plain, Sweaborg was literally wrapt in fire and brimstone, and sulphureous vapours; the glare showed men like ants hurrying to and fro, but not apparently attempting to subdue the flames, which indeed were a hopeless task. Our shells, too, were still falling; and beautiful objects they were, in the dark, mounting up with a twinkling fuse, and descending with a rapid rush and bright explosion. What a change from the early morning; the fortress which then looked so quiet and beautiful was now a veritable seething hell!

I turned in at 1 a.m., and was up at 5, but already the bombardment had been resumed in full blast by the gun and mortar boats, for more than an hour. The fortress presented the same dismal mass of flame and smoke, and where not blazing was smouldering.

The Imperial Standard, which had hitherto floated defiantly from the Citadel, had now disappeared with the Grand Duke, who had posted off in alarm and disgust to St Petersburg, to tell the Czar (as afterwards transpired) that Cronstadt was quite as open to destruction, from our frightful mortar fire, as Sweaborg.

As the second day wore on, our mortar fire perceptibly slackened, not indeed to give the Russians more breathing time, but for the very sufficient reason that the mortars themselves, from long continued firing, were giving in.

The Russian fire, too, was slower and much more deliberate, as they had found random firing was of no avail; and, indeed, many of their guns had been dismounted, and even the casemated forts much knocked about. The mortar practice was now chiefly directed against the Svartos, on which the dockyards and naval establishments were mostly situated. At mid-day a large gas tank in West Svarto blew up, and immediately afterwards the dockyard began to blaze. As the conflagration extended through vast stacks of timber, and stores of tar, pitch, and rosin, it became exceeding fierce. During the afternoon the French rock battery shelled the dockyard and shipping in the harbour, with the greatest precision and most destructive effect. Towards evening several of our mortars had become unserviceable, and even the 68 pounders on the gunboats were showing signs of overwork. The Russian fire continued irregular and ineffective. When darkness came on, a number of boats went in to give the enemy a few parting salvos of fiery rockets, and to set on fire anything not yet ignited. This so annoyed the Russians that, in sheer desperation, they brought cross lights to bear between the shores of Backholm and Helsingfors, in the vain hope of finding the boats. In the evening a final explosion took place on Svarto (west), which set the whole island ablaze, so that by midnight it was a perfect sheet of flame. The bombardment after 9 p.m. gradually subsided, and the last shell was fired about 3 a.m. on Saturday the 11th, the attack having thus continued without cessation for forty-four hours.

Thus ended the greatest exploit of the Allied Baltic Fleet; and it but remains to estimate not only the material but the moral results of perhaps the heaviest naval bombardment on record.

As far as the Allies were concerned it was a very bloodless affair, for, according to Grant, there was not a single man killed, and only 110 wounded. I did not record the numbers in my Journal, beyond that a Lieutenant, a Mate, a Paymaster, and 33 men were wounded in the blockships which were engaged at Sandhamn. At all events, I can vouch not a single man belonging to the "Duke" engaged in the mortar and gun boats was wounded.

The Russians made every endeavour to conceal their losses, which, in killed and wounded, were afterwards ascertained to have been not less than 3,000 men.

Gauged merely by the "butcher's bill," the bombardment was not therefore a terrible fight; yet, it was one of the most telling blows the Russians received during the entire war. Although Sweaborg was virtually destroyed, yet, as the impossible feat of actually capturing it was not attempted, the Russians claimed a repulse which was duly celebrated by a thanksgiving "Te Deum" in St Petersburg and Moscow. Indeed, if the mendacity of the Russian authorities during the war was always shameless, disgraceful, and sometimes almost laughable, it was never more unblushing than in connection with the bombardment of Sweaborg. For downright lying it beat even the Russian record; and the public mind at home was at the time too intent upon the final struggle at Sebastopol either to gauge aright the Russian mendacity, or grasp the full significance and importance of the operations against Sweaborg.

The value of property destroyed, in and about the fortress, amounting to many mill'on roubles, was all the more galling in that it was effected in spite of the enormous fortifications, and a defending force of 40,000 men, and with but trifling loss to the assailants.

But, as afterwards came out, the great material loss was as nothing to the moral effect. The ruin wrought at Sweaborg by our mortar fire brought home to the Czar and his advisers the certainty, that, if the war went on, Cronstadt would next year meet with a similar fate. If that happened, and St Petersburg was menaced, not all the official lying in the world could conceal it from the Russian public. There is the best ground for inferring that the bombardment of Sweaborg was a more important factor in ending the war than even the fall of Sebastopol itself. If the Allies had had a sufficient supply of mortars Cronstadt might have there and then been served as Sweaborg. But the condition of our means of attack may be judged from the following facts: of our sixteen mortars, two were completely split, eight dangerously cracked, and the remainder practically useless from various defects; all were, in fact, used up; several of the long 68 pounders in the gunboats were unfit for service. It was the long continued and incessant firing which wrought such results, which can be estimated by the following statistics: our mortars threw 3,100 shells, or 1,000 tons of iron; and the gunboats fired 12,000 shot and shell. The French probably expended about half that quantity, so that a total of about 25,000 missiles, including rockets, were hurled against Sweaborg. The Russian return fire could hardly have been less, and was probably more. In the thirty daylight hours, during which the bombardment continued, the guns and mortars discharged on either side averaged between twenty and thirty a minute, which will convey some idea of the furious nature of the engagement.

When we turned out on the morning of the 11th the silence around, after the awful turmoil of the preceeding days, was absolutely oppressive. The Fleet was entirely quiescent, but devouring fire still raged in Sweaborg, and dense clouds of smoke rolled eastward before the westerly breeze. Our vessels were all hauled out of range, and the boats repairing damages. Our own gunboat, the "Starling," had been hit twice, and her rail on one side quite carried away. The water around us was now literally covered with empty wooden shell boxes, which had been pitched overboard during the bombardment; the man who could have secured these boxes had a fortune to his hand. During the day, as the fires died down, and the smoke cleared away, the visible damage revealed in Sweaborg was even greater than we expected. The great frowning casemated forts (upon which the Russians were now freely showing themselves), if somewhat battered, were still intact; but the bulk of the open forts and earthworks were mere heaps of rubbish. Everything in the shape of houses were gutted, and only blackened walls left. The great dockyard and vast accumulations of marine stores, and even ships in the harbour were burning. Everything, in fact, really destructible in Sweaborg had succumbed to explosions and conflagrations.

On the same evening the French vessel, "Pelican," left with dispatches for the Allied Governments. I remarked in my Journal—"The news (of the bombardment) will reach London on the 13th, in time to accompany the Queen on her visit to Paris."

On the 12th, the ships were busy getting in topmasts, which had been struck before the bombardment, in readiness for a naval engagement should the Russians have brought out their fleet. Sweaborg was still burning, and had thus been on fire for 64 hours. Great numbers of Russians were seen busy saving property, and repairing some damages, while a large party removed powder from a magazine in dangerous proximity to Helsingfors. One of our satellites, the pleasure yacht "Wee Pet," in spying about, imprudently ventured near the batteries, and getting becalmed would soon have been destroyed had not a gunboat gone to her rescue. Not less than fifty shot and shell were fired at the little intruder, but she was not hit.

The weather, which during the bombardment was all we could desire, now became unsettled; and on the 13th, in rain and mist, the entire fleet, with the exception of the blockships, bade adieu to Sweaborg, and sailed back to Nargen.

CHAPTER XIII.

POST BOMBARDMENT.

AT noon on the 13th we were back at the old anchorage, which we had quitted seven days before. Although 45 miles distant from Sweaborg, the ships at Nargen distinctly heard the sound of the bombardment throughout, and the firing at times seemed so furious that they concluded the line of battle ships were engaging the batteries. At night they also saw the glare of the conflagration. It is needless to say the ships, both here and at Cronstadt, were very jealous of those which had taken part in the bombardment.

The 15th being the Emperor Napoleon III.'s birthday, the French ships were, of course, very gaily be-flagged, and royal salutes were fired at noon and at sunset.

During the next few days several of the disabled mortar boats left for England, from which we inferred that the fighting for this year was over, but I remarked in my Journal—" Next year we will cover the Gulf of Finland with these delightful little craft!" The weather continuing very fine, we went ashore every day for cricket matches and other games.

On the 19th, the mail from Dantzic arrived, bringing a copy of the famous, or rather infamous official "Invalide Russe," with an account of the bombardment of Sweaborg. It was hard to say whether it more amused than astonished us. The strength, position, and extreme violence of the fire from the Allied vessels were given with fair accuracy; but, notwithstanding, wound up with the astounding pious fib, "Thank God, we have received no injury!" For sheer, unblushing official mendacity, that statement took the cake, but, of course, it was meant for consumption in the interior of Russia. Its barefaced impudence must surely have dumfoundered the many thousands about Helsingfors who witnessed the bombardment with their own eyes. The sad condition of the Russian public press then, as probably still, existing, is well illustrated from a conversation which my linguistic friend, Potts, had one day in my presence with an intelligent Nargen islander. The man was fully aware, and admitted that we had smashed up Sweaborg, and that the "Invalide" lied; but when questioned of matters outside his direct knowledge, his ignorance of current events was supreme. He had never heard of Alma, Inkermann, or Balacklava, and shaking his head said—"Only rich men and great readers are allowed to have the newspapers." He had heard of Russian successes—never of defeats. He was asked why it was, since the Russians had so many fine ships at Cronstadt and Sweaborg, which he had seen, they allowed us to blockade them, and did not come out and fight? He replied intelligently—"Ah, you have steam;" but added, "if there had only been French ships they would have come out and fought them steam and all." This, although flattering to us, we assured him was probably a mistake, as our gallant allies were not to be despised either on sea or shore; but it showed the dread in which the British tar is held.

On the 20th, Admiral Baynes arrived from Cronstadt, and reported that on several occasions during the bombardment of Sweaborg the Russians made a show with their steam liners and gunboats as of coming outside the fortifications; but invariably skulked back when they saw the blockading squadron were only but too anxious to meet them. They had no stomach for a naval engagement, at all events with a British Fleet.

The next few days were very stormy, which made us think summer was breaking up; but we went ashore every day to pick the blaeberries, rasps, and crans which grew in the greatest abundance. One day Potts, D'Albertanson, and myself found a stock of cut wood in a remote part of the island, with which we promptly made a fire, and during luncheon warmed ourselves at the Czar's expense.

On the 26th, a French vessel arrived with 20 000 rockets of a new and formidable description, which, it was said, carried a 30 lb. shell effectively up to 7000 yards. We were very anxious they should be tried on Revel, but for some reason they were not. The mail of this date brought the news of the battle of the Tchernaia, in the Crimea, which redounded so much to the credit of the Sardinians.

On the 27th, salutes were fired in honour of Prince Albert's birthday.

On the same day, the spies, which the French had employed to visit and report on Sweaborg, returned. Their account, which was afterwards confirmed through other sources, was a strange commentary on the "Thank God" of the "Invalide

Russe." They were Fins—brothers—caught by the French near Sweaborg, and landed with a promise that if they brought a true account of what they should find there, they would have their boat and belongings returned, together with a handsome present. They consented, after some hesitation, declaring that the mission was full of danger. They now reported that access to Sweaborg was not allowed without special permission, but that they ultimately succeeded in visiting it. The wreck and ruin was awful. All the buildings, and everything inflammable was burned. The number killed was estimated at 2,300, of which 600 were workmen employed on an underground magazine, who were entirely overwhelmed by the great explosion at mid-day on the 9th. Eighteen steamers, or hulks, were sunk or burned. On the first day, a shell went right through the decks of a three decker, lying behind Svarto, exploding and tearing away part of her port broadside; to prevent sinking she was hauled on to a sand bank, but foundered, after all, on an attempt to refloat her. The Russians made great efforts to conceal their losses. Many of the forts were seriously shaken and shattered, and Helsingfors was full of wounded men.

During the next few days it was rumoured that Revel would be attacked; but the wish was father to the thought, in a desire to test the new French rockets. The steady departure of our smaller craft, homeward, clearly negatived any intention of another bombardment.

On the 31st, the "Driver" arrived from Ledsund, in the Gulf of Bothnia, and recounted the following dramatic story:—While she and the

"Dragon" were cruising among the dangerous shoals and islets near Aaland, and were towing some of their manned boats, two belonging to the "Dragon" broke loose during a sudden squall, of which one—a cutter with two men—rapidly drifted out of sight. The poor fellows soon found themselves alone, and approaching a barren rock, on which was a shed, but no inhabitants. When they saw the boat was bound to be dashed to pieces, one said to the other: "I won't die miserably, Jack, I'll try once for life," and jumping overboard, succeeded, bruised and battered, in reaching the rock. His comrade stuck to the boat and was drowned. The survivor, wet, weak, and without food or drink, remained in the shed for two days; and on the second day a boat with four men arrived, but the inhuman wretches, spite his pitiful entreaties, would neither give him bite nor sup, or even allow him to enter their boat.

Just, however, as they shoved off, and he felt going mad, he espied two of his own ship's boats approaching in search of him. He hailed them, and quickly told the tale of the scoundrels who had just left. They immediately started in pursuit, and soon made them prisoners. The great hairy cowards, who were Ledsund fishermen, were now brought for the Admiral's disposal; and, knowing their crime, were in a terrible funk of swinging from a yard arm, which in less squeamish days would have been their fate, and not more than their due. But, instead, their gross inhumanity brought them a sound flogging before release.

The first few days in September were exceedingly fine; and we made the most of them on shore in cricket matches, and other amusements.

The Fleet was now dispersing in twos and

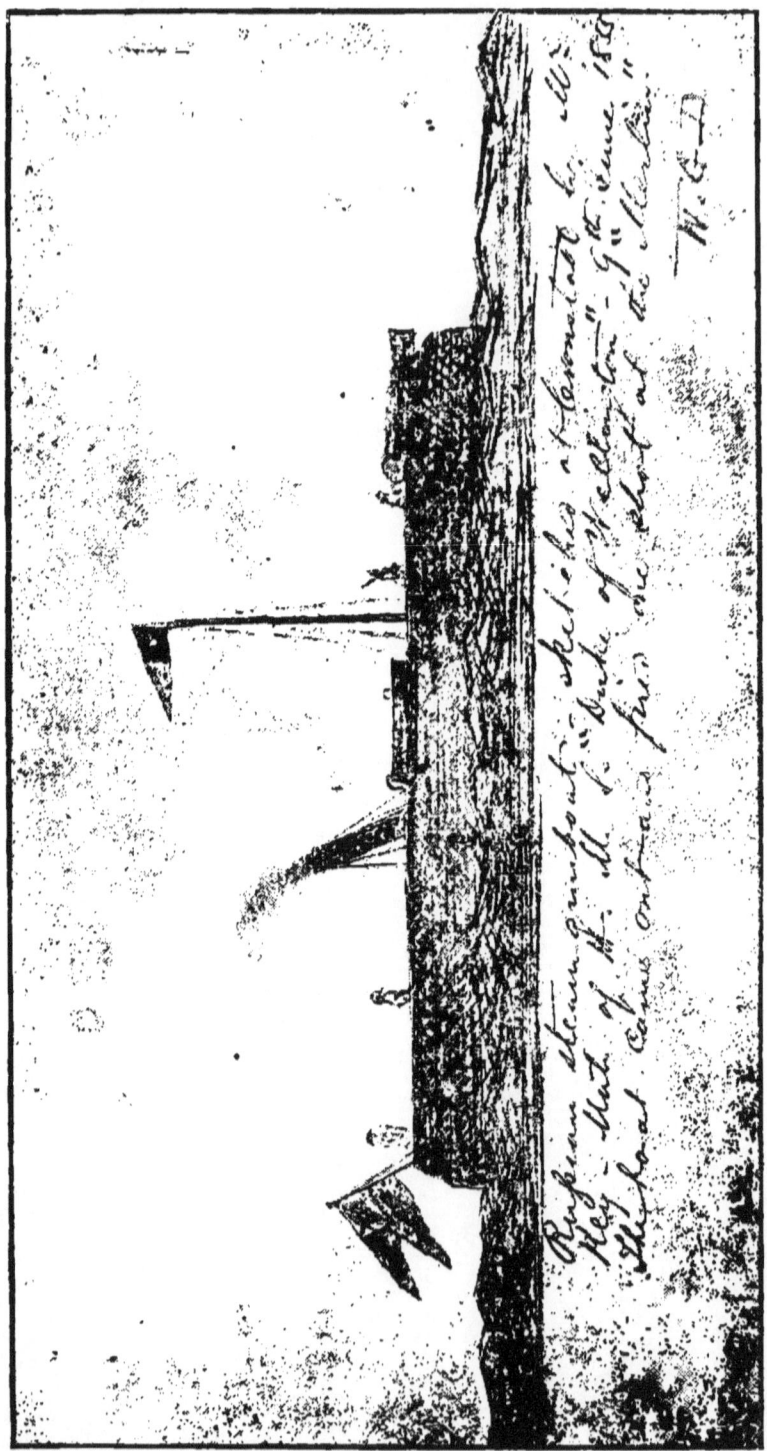

threes homewards; for winter sets in early in these high latitudes, and many of our small craft were hardly suited to face autumn gales, either in the Baltic or the North Sea.

We heard from Cronstadt that, as it happened, on the 2nd only two ships, the "Colossus" 80, and the "Imperieuse" 50 guns, were left blockading the place; the Russians, thinking a chance had come, waxed valiant; and presently a screw liner, a screw frigate, two large paddlewheels, and six steam gunboats, emerged from behind the forts; but instead of our ships retiring before this superior force, they cleared for action and advanced to meet it. Can it be credited, although five to one, the courage of the enemy oozed out of their boots, and they at once turned tail and slunk back under the forts! Could there be any better evidence of the wholesome fear inspired by the unconquered British tar?

On the 5th, a number of boatmen, separately made prisoners near Sweaborg, were brought in and examined apart, and independently, as to the effects of the bombardment, and the after condition of the fortress. Their testimony was very unanimous, and fully confirmatory of the news brought by the French spies.

On the 6th, More and I made official application for a passage home, in accordance with instructions received from the Admiralty.

On the 7th, we got a large quantity of cucumbers and pumpkins from Revel, through Nargen. Although they were very acceptable, some of our wags declared they were only sent to give us the cholera!

On the 8th, we played a grand cricket match—

"The 'Duke' v. The Fleet," and had the satisfaction of winning by 101 against 56 in one innings, being unable to pull off a second. Our little "Starling" arrived from Sweaborg with Mr Crowe, Swedish Interpreter, on board. He landed disguised, and after gathering much information, entirely confirmatory of all we had heard regarding the bombardment, was somehow recognized and chased by Cossacks, But for the kindness of a Swedish family he would probably have been caught, and ——?

On the 9th a number of manned boats, under Captain Caldwell of the "Duke," chased and captured several "cut wood" boats, making for Revel, at a place called Wolf Island. A Russian gentleman came off in a boat, and remonstrated with Caldwell, but said he would sell the wood if we wanted it. Our gallant skipper only laughed at his impudence, and told him if he did not take himself off, he would buy him cheap—as a prisoner! These little interchange of courtesies were carried on in French.

On the 13th, through the death of the Paymaster of the "Vulture," our most popular and worthy messmate, Assistant Paymaster Bone, was advanced a step in rank, which we duly celebrated with much enthusiasm, especially as he was not to leave the ship, having been at once appointed to the Admiral's Office.

During these days I was constantly recording gales of wind, and furious squalls, which clearly indicated the break up of the summer.

On the 14th, a blue jacket was flogged for being drunk on duty. How sailors frequently manage to get drunk on board ship, even when lying off an enemy's coast, and under strict discipline, is one of these puzzles of which I have never heard any consistent or satisfactory explanation.

On the 17th, the mail arrived from Dantzic with the glorious news of the Fall of Sebastopol. Although, of course, deeply and chiefly concerned in the part we were ourselves playing in the war, we remained much interested in the progress of events in the Crimea.

The great news was received with much rejoicing; the ships were decorated; grand salutes were fired, and extra grog served out all round. If the news had not already reached Revel, the excitement in the Fleet must have told them something big had happened.

The festivities that were planned to celebrate the victory fell flat, so far as More and I were concerned, by the receipt of sudden and unexpected orders, at 2 p.m., to at once proceed on board the blockship " Cornwallis" for passage home. Homeward bound, although always of pleasant sound, did not then exactly fit into our immediate plans. We quickly packed up—not a difficult matter, our limited belongings. Our sea chests were hoisted out of the cockpit, and with our hammocks speedily placed in a boat alongside.

Then, with a parting glass, and a warm good-bye to messmates, and many friends, both officers and men, at 4 p.m. we quitted the dear old " Duke." and the happy associations connected therewith. My eyes were filled with tears; for I had spent, in happiness and comfort, exactly 174 days on board; free from quarrel, or scarcely a passing difference with either officer or man. Since then, in the army and civil life, I have been blessed with many friendships, pleasant at the time, and full of happy memories; yet, on a retrospect, I feel assured that nowhere could the youthful *camaraderie* be excelled which existed in such a place, and under such circumstances as fell to my lot in the Gun Room, and Cockpit of the "Duke of Wellington."

CHAPTER XIV.

HOMEWARD BOUND.

OUR first thoughts on board the "Cornwallis" were: what a change is here! We had fallen back half a century, and, as it were, passed by a step from a modern mansion to an old dingy tenement! This ancient man o' war was indeed a contrast to the spaciously built, and elaborately fitted up-to-date three decker we had just quitted. For this so-called blockship (derivation unrevealed) was simply an old-fashioned 74 gun two decker, lightened aft by removal of the poop (which gave her an odd, shorn appearance) to admit of fitting in a high pressure auxiliary engine, with reduction of armament to 60 guns. The combination in the blockships of the screw, propellor, and heavy sailing rig was incongruous; the more so when under steam, as the high pressure engines puffed and snorted like locomotives. Yet, while sense adversely contrasted the old with the new, sentiment restored the balance; for, were not these uncouth blockships but transformed "Seventy-fours," the very type of ship which, from Rodney to Nelson, covered the British Navy with everlasting renown? It was " the thunders from their native oak" that did not merely quench the enemy above, but "quell the floods below." The "Cornwallis" was undoubtedly very old, for her huge and clumsy wooden "knees" dated her construction back to the early years of the century. Yet, ancient or no, she could boast, with nineteen shot holes received at Sweaborg, of being the fighting ship of the whole Baltic Fleet. These holes in her sides, rudely plugged, as well as her ripped-up decks, roughly patched, were objects of much curiosity to me; as representing such scars as must have been common in the days when "hearts of oak were our ships, jolly tars were our men." One of the shots she received went right through the cooking galley, while dinner was being prepared, wastefully scattering the pea soup and salt junk all over the deck! On second thoughts, therefore, one felt proud of the venerable "Cornwallis," and of sailing in a ship identical with those that won Trafalgar. The old world associations of the ship appeared to react on the crew, among whom there was little of the modern smartness we had been accustomed to on the "Duke."

On board we found about half-a-dozen "Doctor's Mates" on passage home like ourselves. They were mostly London men, and did not impress either More or myself favourably.

She sailed about 8 p.m., the band playing "Homeward Bound;" and so, amid great rejoicing, and gathering night, we said good-bye to the Baltic Fleet.

As both steaming and sailing, we could not get more than $3\frac{1}{2}$ knots out of the old tub, it took three days to get to Faro, which the "Duke" could have covered in one. But our after progress was better, along the coasts of Gothland. Bornholm, and the southern Swedish peninsula; so that, at 8 a.m. on the 23d, we anchored, in good weather, 8 miles from Copenhagen; at 5 p.m. we passed up the Sound to Elsinore, where we anchored at 9 p.m.

As we were to be two days there, and had nothing to do, we determined to see as much as possible. We therefore left in a passenger steamer in the morning for Copenhagen, which we reached before mid-day, landing at the entrance of the river-like channel, which divides the town into two parts connected by drawbridges. I was greatly interested in this fine Royal city of 150,000 inhabitants: not merely on account of its picturesque streets—new and old—but by reason of its associations with Nelson and the famous battle of the Baltic. The harbour lies between Copenhagen proper and Christianshaven on the island of Amager, and shelters the Danish naval establishments and fleet. We drove along the fine street, called after the Goths—Gothers-gade—to the Phoenix Hotel; when lo! lounging on the steps of that hostelry was the inevitable Continental Englishman! In this instance he proved to be a Scotsman, partly tourist and partly semi-resident, who welcomed us as if old friends, and volunteered to pilot us over the sights of the town.

After luncheon we started in open carriages, driving round the town and fortifications, and visiting the Museum, University, &c., but especially the grand old Rosenberg Palace, which contains many curious and priceless national treasures. The keeper was a very voluble old fellow, who spoke English well; and, as we were not reckoned everybody, showed us privately the extraordinary iron branks, bracelets, armlets, leglets, and waistbands with which the Vikings of old secured their female kind before starting on a piratical expedition. The old heathen rovers had evidently little confidence in the honour of their women; and the torture of wearing such horrid fetters, for perhaps months on end, must have been terrible. The names of the "gades" (streets) seemed quite familiar to me, and strongly recalled the "Overgate," "Seagate," &c., of Dundee. The beautiful cemetery, just outside the walls, was doubly interesting, because, over the entrance was the homely word "Kirkyeord," and inside, the British and Danish killed, in the bombardment of 1801, sleep peacefully side by side. After making a few purchases, including the fine transparent porcelain lamp shades for which the town is famous, and having treated our guide, we left by the steamer about six o'clock, and reached our own ship before nine.

The following day we explored Elsinore and its neighbourhood, but did not find much of interest. It is a very quaint place, with an old Castle, or Kronberg, which, by some stretch of the imagination, is supposed to control the Sound—here about $3\frac{1}{2}$ miles wide to the Swedish mainland. At that time the "Sound Dues," an extraordinary survival of the exactions of the Vikings, were still levied, and for their enforcement a number of revenue cutters were lying under the Castle.

As there was little to see in the town we struck into the country to visit "Hamlet's Grave," some two miles away. We searched in vain for it for some time, and our enquiries in English, of the wayside peasants, only met with a shake of the head. At length, in a happy moment, I bethought me of my mother tongue, and asked in broad Scotch: "Whaur Hamlet yirdit?" This at once brought a pleased "ja, ja" from a man, who conducted us to a few stunted trees, fenced with an iron railing. This spot was supposed to be the last resting place of the moody "Prince of Denmark;" but whether or not, it was so bare and utterly devoid of romance that we soon hurried back to Elsinore.

On the 26th, we entered the Categat and rounded the Schaw, heading southward, and so bade final farewell to the Baltic. The rough seas and the greenish water soon showed we had left the brackish land-locked basin; and our progress became sadly poor. The old ship, short in length and broad in beam, rolled and pitched like an egg: so that I wished our course had been the short westward one for Aberdeen.

But the North Foreland was our object point; and so, after some days, of no little discomfort, and a good deal of sea sickness, we at last sighted the white cliffs of Kent.

We arrived at Portsmouth on the 3rd, and disembarked—bag and baggage—on the 4th. My naval service thus lasted 6 months and 6 days; and I for one never had any cause to regret these experiences.

At the Custom House, I learned, through my friend, Mr Maclean, of the death of my beloved sister Jeannie (Mrs Hood) on the 15th September. This blow, although not altogether unexpected, sadly marred my landing.

I immediately got into plain clothes, and crammed my uniform and effects into my sea chest and dispatched it home. Some of my companions disposed of their kit, but I was determined my mother should see mine.

According to instructions, we immediately proceeded to London, and personally reported our arrival at the Admiralty. Our reception by the Medical Director General was kindly, and he offered several of us commissions in the navy, for the asking, after we had duly qualified. My friend Lees, and several others afterwards availed themselves of the offer. We were each then presented with a douceur of £25—which, together with what I had saved from my pay, made me feel richer than ever before!

I then hurried home to Scotland, where I was received with own arms by relatives and friends; and in my native neighbourhood found myself a bit of a hero. My sea kit and warlike trophies were objects of admiration; and my tales the subject of earnest interrogation and wonder.

At the end of October we again forgathered at the point from which we had started, in Edinburgh; and there, on many occasions, both quiet and festive, fought our Baltic battles "o'er again." In due course during the winter we were delighted to receive the Baltic Medal, with our names and ships engraved round the rim. To those who afterwards entered the Army and Navy this was a decoration from the day on which we donned our uniform.

These reminiscences are forty years old; and belong to a period since which everything naval has been almost totally revolutionized. Never again can anyone be called upon to serve in a great, oaken three decker; and not only are the ships and conditions of warfare totally changed, but even the men are different—whether for the better or the worse it is not for me to say.

In a very short time the wooden walls of old England will be a mere memory to the aged, and a tradition to all others. It is just, therefore, because the naval world of 1855, into which I have let some light, can never re-emerge, that I venture to hope these short personal chronicles may in future time possess some interest, long after the actors therein, myself included, have passed away, and, as living men, are altogether forgotten.

APPENDIX.

SOME OF OUR BALTIC GUNROOM SONGS.

THE POPE.

(Sung by Robert Bone.)

The Pope he leads a happy life,
He has no care nor wedded strife,
He drinks the best of Rhenish wine,
I would the Pope's gay life were mine!

Yet, his is not a family house,
He has no cheery, loving spouse;
No child has he to bless his hope,
I wouldn't wish to be the Pope.

The Sultan better pleases me,
He lives a life of jollity;
Has wives as many as he will,
I would the Sultan's throne then fill!

But, yet, he's not a happy man,
He must obey the Al-Koran;
He dare not taste one drop of wine
I would not change his lot for mine.

So here, content, I'll take my stand,
I'll drink my own, my native land;
I'll kiss my maiden's lips divine,
And drink the best of Rhenish wine.

And when my maiden kisses me,
I'll fancy I the Sultan be;
And when my cheering glass I tope,
I'll fancy then I am the Pope!

WHEN THE SWALLOWS HOMEWARD FLY.

(The best translation from the German.)

(Sung by W. G. Don.)

When the swallows homeward fly,
When the roses fade and die;
When the nightingale's soft lay,
Warbles at the close of day,
Why fond heart this beating pain,
Why fond heart this beating pain!
If that form no more I see,
Parting from thee, love, is woe to me,
Parting from thee, love, is woe to me.

When the wild swan southward goes,
Where the perfumed citron blows;
Where the glorious evening sun
O'er yon forest green goes down;
   Why fond heart, etc.

Cease, poor heart, no longer mourn,
Joy will soon to thee return;
If I see that face again,
Parting will have lost its pain.
Heart be still, no more repine,
Heart be still, no more repine,
If I see that form once more,
Parting and sadness will then be o'er,
Parting and sadness will then be o'er!

ISLE OF BEAUTY!

(Gunroom Stock Song.)

Shades of evening close not o'er us
  Leave our lonely barque a while;
Morn, alas! will not restore us
  Yonder dim and distant isle.
Still my fancy can discover
  Sunny spots where friends may dwell;
Absence makes the heart grow fonder,
  Isle of Beauty! Fare thee well!

When the shadows round me gather,
  As I pace the deck alone ;
And my eyes in vain are seeking
  Some green spot to rest upon ;
What would I not give to wander
  Where my old companions dwell ;
Absence makes the heart grow fonder,
  Isle of Beauty ! Fare thee well !

HEARTS OF OAK.
(Midshipman Fawkes's Song.)

Come cheer up, my lads, 'tis to glory we steer,
To add something new to this wonderful year ;
To honour we call you, not press you like slaves,
For who are so free as the sons of the waves ?
Hearts of oak are our ships, jolly tars are our men,
We always are ready—steady, boys, steady ;
We'll fight and we'll conquer again and again.

We ne'er see our foes, but we wish them to stay,
They never see us, but they wish us away ;
If they run why we follow, and run them ashore,
And if they won't fight us, we cannot do more.
    Hearts of oak, etc.

They swear they'll invade us, these terrible foes,
They frighten our women, our children, and beaux ;
But should their flat bottoms in darkness get o'er,
Still Britons they'll find to receive them on shore.
    Hearts of oak, etc.

BATTLE OF THE BALTIC.
(Sung by W. G. Don.)

Of Nelson and the north,
  Sing the glorious days' renown ;
When to battle fierce came forth
  All the might of Denmark's crown ;
And their arms along the deep proudly shone ;
    By each gun a lighted brand,
    In a bold determined hand,
  And the Prince of all the Land
Led them on.

Like Leviathans afloat
  Lay our bulwarks on the brine ;
While the sign of battle flew
  'Long the lofty British line ;
It was ten of April morn by the chime ;
  As they drifted on their path
  There was silence deep as death,
  And the boldest held his breath
For a time.

But the might of England flushed
  To anticipate the scene ;
While her van the fleeter rushed
  O'er the deadly space between ;
"Hearts of oak !" our captains cried, when each gun,
  From its adamantine lips,
  Spread a death shade round the ships,
  Like the hurricane eclipse
Of the sun.

Again, again, again,
  And the havoc did not slack ;
Till a feeble cheer the Dane
  To our cheering sent us back ;
And their shots along the deep slowly boom,
  Then ceased ; and all is wail
  As they strike the shattered sail,
  Or in conflagration pale
Light the gloom.

Brave hearts to Britain's pride
  Once so faithful and so true,
On the deck of fame that died
  With the gallant, good Riou ;
Soft sigh the winds of heaven o'er their grave ;
  While the billow mournful rolls,
  And the mermaids' song condoles,
  Singing glory to the souls
Of the brave.

Now joy, Britannia raise
  For the tidings of thy might,
By the festal city's blaze
  While the wine cup shines in light ;
But yet amid that joy and uproar ;
  Let us think of them that sleep,
Full many a fathom deep,
  By thy wild and stormy steep
Elsinore !

―――>><<―――

BRITANNIA, THE QUEEN OF THE OCEAN.

(General Chorus—An old song revived, and adapted to the French Alliance.)

O Britannia, the pride of the ocean,
  The home of the brave and the free ;
The shrine of each seaman's devotion,
  What land can compare unto thee !
Thy banners make heroes assemble
  When Liberty's form meets their view,
Thy mandates make Tyranny tremble,
  When borne by the Red, White, and Blue.
    When borne by the Red, White, and Blue,
    When borne by the Red, White, and Blue,
  Thy mandates make Tyranny tremble,
    When borne by the Red, White, and Blue.

Where war scattered wild desolation,
  And threaten'd our isle to deform,
The ark then of Freedom's foundation,
  Britannia rode safe through the storm ;
With her flag floating gaily before her,
  As proudly she bore her brave crew,
With her unconquered flag before her,
  The flag of the Red, White, and Blue.
    The flag, etc.

The wine cup of union bring hither,
  And fill it right up to the brim ;
May the wreaths of our heroes ne'er wither,
  Nor the star of their glories grow dim.
May the France from old England ne'er sever,
  But each to their colours prove true,
And while crushing the Tyrant for ever,
  Give three cheers for the Red, White, and Blue.
    Three cheers for the Red, White, and Blue,
    Three cheers for the Red, White, and Blue,
    The Army and Navy for ever,
    Three cheers for the Red, White, and Blue.

THE BOMBARDMENT OF SWEABORG.

(Composed by the Hon. Augustus C. Hobart, naval commander of the Mortar Boats, and Frederick Hill, Esq., Russian Interpreter. Tune—"Villikins," then popular through the famous Sam Cowell. Sung with great applause throughout the Fleet.)

An Imperial* Grand Duke once to Sweaborg came down,
To inspect the defences of that famous town ;
Of infernal machines he had laid down ten score,
But thought he might find room for one or two more.
    Singing Tooral i tooral, i tooral i lay, etc.

'Twas the 9th day of August—one quarter past six,
When De Berg† to the palace came running like bricks,
Said he, " Please your Highness, Dundas and Penaud
Have come with their mortars and gunboats in tow."
    Singing Tooral, etc.

" Well, come then, De Berg," this young Grand Duke said he,
" To sink all these vessels would be a fine spree ;
We'll soon let these infidel Britishers know
That to trifle with us and with Sweaborg's no go."
    Singing Tooral, etc. (swaggering chorus.)

He had scarce said the words when he heard a great squall,
For our mortar and gunboats had opened the ball ;
A thirteen inch shell pitched on to the roof
Of the Great Magazine, which was not quite bomb proof.
    Singing Tooral, etc. (for the shell.)

* Constantine, Lord High Admiral of Russia.
† General De Berg commanding the Army of Finland.

The explosion was awful as Constantine found,
When he saw his brave soldiers lying dead all around ;
The fire it was spreading right in his direction,
So he thought he'd be off, or 'twould spoil his complexion.
    Singing Tooral, etc. (to assist rising fire.)

He sent for his Generals there on the Staff,
And told them he feared we were too strong by half ;
Said he, " I am off,* but I'll send you relief,
And I hope most sincerely you won't come to grief."
    Singing Tooral, etc.

The grief that he spoke of, alas ! too soon came.
For the Rooshians soon found we'd the best of the game ;
Our shot and our shell so knocked them about,
That the whole place was soon turned inside out.
    Singing Tooral, etc. (melancholy for gutted Sweaborg.)

This game we kept up for full two days and more,†
Till in Sweaborg's great fortress we left not a store ;
And proved to the Rooshians 'twas not true as said,
That the Fleet in the Baltic could only blockade.
    Singing Tooral, etc. (powerfully for Baltic Fleet.)

    Morial—Specially for the Grand Duke.

O Constantine, Constantine, mind what I say,
With the English and French Fleets no dodges to play,
You thought you could sink us by infernal‡ machines,
But another time you'd better try fairer means.
    Singing Tooral, etc. (grand and imposing for alike speedy destruction of the hornet nests.

* Polted, ostensibly to get relief, but really to inform the Czar that Cronstadt was in danger.
† Bombardment lasted 44 hours, from 7 a.m. on the 9th, to 4 a.m. on 11 h August.
‡ Reckoned then despicable foul play.

INDEX.

Abramsholm, French battery on - - - - 92
Accidents, on board - - - - - 53, 72, 84
Admiralty, Lords' inspection - - - - - 27
,,   offer to Volunteers - - - - 10
,,   reporting at - - - - - 13, 120
Advance, Pay - - - - - - - 14
Aldershot, Camp - - - - - - - 15
Allied Baltic Fleet, list of - - - - 86-87-88

Baird, Lieutenant - - - - - - - 45
Baltic Fleet 1854-5 - - - - - - - 9
,,   ,,   crews of - - - - - - 26
,,   ,,   function of - - - - - - 57
,,   ,,   gunpowder in - - - - - 86
,,   ,,   list of - - - - - - - 86-88
,,   ,,   medical men for - - - - - 9, 10
,,   mirage - - - - - - - 63, 69
Banks, Assistant Surgeon - - - - - 45
Barnardiston, Lieutenant - - - - - 45
Bells, ship's - - - - - - - 37-39
Biorka, affair at - - - - - - 83
Blaeberries, at Nargen - - - - - 84-85, 108
Boatman, drunken - - - - - - 25
,,   Long - - - - - - - 31
Bone, Paymaster - - - - - - 47, 112
Bornholm, island - - - - - - 54, 116
Breakfast, on Board - - - - - - 38
British, Sailors - - - - - - 39-40, 42
"Britannia," Collier - - - - - - 55
Broadside of Fleet - - - - - - 26

Caldwell, Captain - - - - 18, 44, 86, 112
Camperdown, sail past - - - - - 51
Canterbury Hall - - - - - - 14

Capture of Russian Boats - - - - 66, 78, 112
Cargill, David —Master - - - - - 55
Cattegat - - - - - - - 52, 119
Channel Fleet - - - - - - 50
Cleaning Decks - - - - - - 23, 38
Cockpit, life in - - - - - 35-36, 114
Coghill, Friend - - - - - - 12, 14
Collision with Emigrants' Ship - - - - 28-29
Continental Englishman, the - - - - - 117
Copenhagen, visit to - - - - - 117-118
Cornwallis, description of - - - - 115
  ,,   shots in - - - - - - 116
Cowell, Sam - - - - - - - 14
Crews of Fleet - - - - - - 26-27
Cricket matches - - - - - 110, 111-2
Cronstadt, advance to - - - - - 65-67
  ,,   anchor off - - - - - 67
  ,,   description of - - - - - 68
  ,,   during bombardment of Sweaborg - 108, 111
  ,,   easterly gale at - - - - - 77
  ,,   forts of - - - - - - 68
  ,,   garrison of - - - - - 68
  ,,   infernal machines at - - - 72, 76
  ,,   leave - - - - - - 80
  ,,   Russian Fleet in - - - 67-68, 70
  ,,   reconnoitring by Admiral - - 69-70
  ,,   shell practice at - - - - 78, 79
  ,,   shots fired into - - - - 79-80
  ,,   visitors from St Petersburg - - 75, 79
Crowe, "Jim" - - - - - - - 49
Cut wood boats - - - - - - 66, 112

Days, number on board Duke - - - - 113
Deaths on board - - - - - 52, 53, 63
Decks, scrubbing of - - - - - 23, 38
Deserters - - - - - - - 70, 79
Dinner hours - - - - - - - 39
Director General, Medical - - - - 13, 120
Divisions, ship's - - - - - - 38-39
Doctors' Mates - - - - - - 10, 116
Domville, Surgeon - - - - - - 45
Douceurs, money - - - - - - 120
Dover, heights of - - - - - - 29
Downs, The - - - - - - 29, 50

Drills, special	40
Duke, cable of	27, 50
,, collision of	28
,. description of	31-36
Duncan, Assistant Surgeon	18, 31, 45, 61
Dundas, Admiral Sir R. S.	9, 43, 69
Eden, Midshipman	48
Edinburgh, leave	12
,, return to	120
Elsinore, anchor at	117
,, Hamlet's grave	118-9
,, visit to	118
Embark, for duty	22
Enemy, chase of	65-66
Faro island	55, 63, 116
,, women of	55
,, small-pox hospital at	55
Fawkes, Midshipman	47
Fins, prisoners	80, 109-110-111
Finland, Gulf of	54, 56, 64, 106
Flag ship, appointment to	13
Fleet, list of	86-88
Flogging, description of	62-63, 112
Flying Squadron	54, 56
Frederickshaven, affair at	85
French, Emperor	50, 84, 106
,, entertainment of	71, 83
,, officers	71, 83
,, rockets	108
,, rock battery at Sweaborg	92-93, 101
,, spies at Sweaborg	108-9
,, Squadron	69, 88
Fun, on board	36, 41, 75
Funeral, at sea	52.
Giraud, Friend	25
Gothland, island	54, 116
Grand Duke Constantine	93, 100
Great Belt	52
Gunboats, description of	89
,, Sweaborg at	92, 96, 101
Gun Room, introduction to	22

Gun Room, life in - - - - - - 34, 114
,, songs of - - - - - 123-129
Guns, on Duke - - - - - - 16-17
Gunpowder in Fleet - - - - - 86
Gustafsvard - - - - - - 91, 92, 98

Hamblin, Marine - - - - - - 22-23
Hamlet's grave, visit to - - - - - 118-9
Hammocks - - - - - 20, 22, 33, 38, 113
Hannen, Lieutenant - - - - - 44, 63, 70
Hango Head, affair of - - - - 71, 74-75
Helsingfors, description of - - - - - 90
Hill, Interpreter - - - - - - 46, 61
Hobart, Lieutenant - - - - - - 44, 70
Homeward bound - - - - - - 115
Hospital Dressers - - - - - - 10

Infernal Machines, discovery of - - - - 72
,, ,, description of - - - - 77
,, ,, explosion of - - - - 72, 76
"Invalide Russe," mendacity of - - - - 107

Join ships - - - - - - - 18
Journal, keeping of - - - - - - 16, 71
Journey to London - - - - - - 12

Kiel, arrive at - - - - - - 52
,, description of - - - - - 53
,, leave - - - - - - 54
,, sail for - - - - - - 51
,, scenes in - - - - - - 53

Leave on shore - - - - - - 25, 30
Ledsund, tragedy at - - - - - 110
Lees, Friend - - - - - - 15, 16, 120
Le Grand, Surgeon - - - - - - 45
Leningen, Prince - - - - - - 78, 87
Liquor on board - - - - - 35, 112
Lockhart, Cadet - - - - - - 48
London, arrive at - - - - - - 12
,, return to - - - - - 119-120
Lords, of Amiralty - - - - - 27

Mackay, Burke and Wheeler - - - - - 14

INDEX. 135

Maclean, Mr - - - - - - 20, 25, 119
Malacca, paddle - - - - - - 25
Marines in Fleet - - - - - 26-27, 42
Master at Arms - - - - - - 36
Marlborough, liner - - - - - - 31
Medals, receipt of - - - - - - 120
Medical Men for Fleet - - - - - 10
Men, number on Board - - - - - 25, 32
Midshipman, Senior - - - - - - 47
Messing, cost of Gun Room - - - - 35
Midsummer in Baltic - - - - - 72, 75
Mirage ,, ,, - - - - - 63, 68
More, Friend James - - 14, 22, 45, 48, 63, 111, 116
Moriarty, Master - - - - - - 45
Mortar boats, account of - - - - - 83. 89
,, ,, damage to - - - - - 103
,, ,, shells of - - - - 95, 97, 100
,, ,, Sweaborg, at - - - 93, 95, 97, 103
Munday, Secretary - - - - - - 46

Napoleon III. - - - - - 50, 64, 106
Nargen Island, cemetery - - - - - 85
,, description of - - - - - 58-59
,, lighthouse of - - - - - 60
,, people of - - - - - 58, 60
,, visits to - - - 56, 58, 60, 83, 84, 108
Narva, bombardment of - - - - - 75
Nelson, relics of - - - - - - 85
Night inspection of ship - - - - - 39
North Sea gale, - - - - - - 51
Nugent, Captain - - - - - - 46

Officers of Duke, - - - - - - 42-49
,, French - - - - - - 71, 83
Onslow, Chaplain - - - - - 24, 34, 46
Orienbaum - - - - - - - 67
Ottershall, island - - - - - - 92

Parker, Mate - - - - - - - 47
Pay, advance of - - - - - - 14
Pelham, Commodore - - - - - - 44
Penaud, Admiral - - - - - - 69
Polish Deserters - - - - - - 70, 71
Portsmouth, description of - - - - 19

Portsmouth, dockyard - - - - - - 31
,,   journey to - - - - - - 14
Portsmouth, leave - - - - - - 28, 50
,,   return to - - - - - 29, 119
,,   scenes in - - - - - 19, 20-21
Pot s. Clerk - - - - - - 48, 53, 107, 108
Preedy, Commander G. W. - - - 22, 44, 61, 89
Provision vessels - - - - - - - 79

Quarters, divisional - - - - - - 38-39
,,   fire - - - - - - - - 40
,,   general - - - - - - 40, 54, 78

Rations, rum - - - - - - - - 35
,,   ship's- - - - - - - - 35
Repairs, after collision - - - - 29-30, 50
Revel, blockade of - - - - - - - 85
,,   description of - - - - - - 58
,,   reconnoitred - - - - - - - 84
Routine of war ship - - - - - - 37-41
Russian Empress, birthday of - - - - 80
,,   dread of British Fleet - - 68, 107, 111
,,   mendacity - - - - - 102, 107
,,   Royal Standard - - - - 92, 100

Sailors, specimens of - - - - - - 32, 42
Sailing of Fleet - - - - - - - 28
Saluting, amenities of - - - - - - 69
Sam's Coffee House- - - - - - - 13
Scott, Friend - - - - - - - 15, 18
Scotland, back to - - - - - - - 120
Sea kit, buying of - - - - - 14, 18, 19-20
Sebastopol, fall of - - - - - - - 113
September, weather in - - - - 110, 112
Seskar, visit to island of - - - - - 73, 82
Ships, choice of - - - - - - - 13
Sickbay - - - - - - - - 24, 28, 37
Sickness, sea - - - - - - - 51, 119
Small-pox - - - 44, 53, 55, 61, 63, 70, 78
Somerset House - - - - - - - 13
Spithead, ships at - - - - - - 17, 25-26
Story, Midshipman - - - - - - 83
St Petersburg - - - - - 63, 69, 100, 102
Sunday, first on board - - - - - 23-24

INDEX. 137

Supplies, abundance of - - - - - - 35 71
Svartos - - - - - - - - 91, 100
Sweaborg, Admiral reconnoitre - - - - 84
,, ammunition expended at - - - 103
,, anchor off - - - - - - 89
,, appearance of - - - - - - 90-91
,, attacking force at - - - - - 92-93
,, bombardment, commencement of - - 95
,, burning of - - - - - 99, 103
,, citadel - - - - - - - 99
,, condition after bombardment - - 104-109
,, Cornwallis hulled at - - - 97, 116
,, departure for - - - - - - 89
,, description of - - - - - 90 91
,, disposition of attack - - - 93
,, explosions in - - - - 97, 98, 100, 101
,, French rock battery at - - 92-93, 101
,, Gunboats, attack on - - - - 96
,, Imperial Standard at - - - 92, 100
,, killed and wounded at - - - 101-2, 109
,, leave - - - - - 105
,, material and moral results at - - - 101-3
,, mortar fire at - - - - 95. 100, 103
,, rocket fire at - - - - 99, 101, 103
,, Russians fire at - - 96, 97. 99, 100, 103
,, spies report on - - - - - 108-9
,, weather during bombardment - - 90, 105
,, "Wee Pet," escape of - - - - 105
Syme, Professor - - - - - - - 10

Tea, meal - - - - - - - - 39
Temperature in Baltic - - 56, 72, 79, 84, 110, 112
Terms of appointment to Fleet - - - - 10
Tolboukin, lighthouse - - - - 67, 75, 78, 80
Travers, Colonel - - - - - - 46, 84
Turn in, hours of - - - - - - - 39

Uniform, getting of - - - - - - - 14

Vargon - - - - - - - 91, 92, 97, 98
Victory. The - - - - - - - 17, 27
Volunteering for Fleet - - - - - - 10

Weather in Baltic - - 56, 72, 79, 84, 89, 110, 112

Ward Room - - . - . - 33, 46, 61, 71
Watches, shipboard - - . . - . 37
Whitecombe, Steward - . . - - 34-35, 83

Yachts, pleasure - . . . . - 93, 105
Yankee Skipper . - . . . - - 29-30
York, scenes at - - — 12

www.ingramcontent.com/pod-product-compliance
Lightning Source LLC
Chambersburg PA
CBHW030258170426
43202CB00009B/791